THE
GOOD
DIVORCE
GUIDE

Suzanne Ruthven
& Paul Harriss

First published in Great Britain by
How To Books 2002

Revised edition published by ignotus press 2005
BCM-Writer, London WC1N 3XX

British Library Cataloguing in Publication Data
ISBN: 1 903768 30 6

Printed in Great Britain by A2 Reprographics
Set in Baskerville Old Face 11pt

NOTE:
The material contained in this book is set out in good faith for
general guidance and no liability can be accepted for loss or
expense incurred as a result of relying in particular circumstances
on statements made in the book. Laws and regulations are complex
and liable to change, and readers should check the current position
with the relevant authorities before making personal arrangements.

Contents

Preface

When we first began discussing the most common reasons why people get divorced, or decide to terminate a long-term relationship, my co-author said: "There are only four real reasons — money, sex, bad behaviour and those who should never have got married in the first place."

"You realise," I replied, "that your comment has effectively scuppered the first four chapters of soul-sister empathising out of the book?"

"Good," came the response, "the last thing men want is a lot of social chit-chat thinly disguised as meaningful dialogue. We want solid, practical advice along the lines of *Go directly to Jail; Do not pass Go; Do not collect £200.*"

Even if you've not actually been through a divorce, most people have a second-hand or one-sided view of divorce that has been gleaned from the media and close friends who have gone through the process. Not to mention Brian down the pub, whose 'wife's cousin got took for a quarter of a million and the house when his missus went off with another bloke'. It's not until we become embroiled in the due process of the law ourselves that we quickly come to realise the *last* thing we need is a bar-room lawyer full of tall tales and horror stories. What we *do* need is constructive advice to guide us through the minefield with the minimum of anxiety, inconvenience and bad feeling. Even with expert guidance, however, there are some things that only we can do for ourselves.

Regardless of the reasons for divorce there is still a tremendous amount of emotional baggage that we need to sort out — and it isn't that easy to just walk away and begin life anew. Coming to terms with the reasons *behind* those cited on the divorce petition can help us to understand what caused the fissures to develop in the first place. In a large number of cases we're looking at plain and simple incompatibility. From the strain of incompatibility the tiny fissures grow into crevices; the crevices widen into chasms until the relationship becomes so unsound that entire edifice crashes to the ground.

In situations such as these, no-one is to blame but the law still demands that one party cites the other's conduct as grounds for divorce. Boredom, weakness, disappointment and unreliability are hardly legitimate grounds; neither can an anti-social, noncommunicative or undemonstrative partner be deemed the villain of the piece just because life has not come up to expectations. It may simply be that the couple have simply stopped loving each other — or what they *thought* was love was never there in the first place.

A family friend who has been married to her second husband for twenty years commented: "I think couples should be married on a licence which is renewable after 10 years with an opt-out clause for either party. It would make life a lot easier and it would stop people from taking each other for granted. It would probably make the marriage stronger because both parties would have to try harder."

It is also important to understand right from the start that whatever our personal opinions might be about the morality or fairness of the divorce business, they account for nothing in the eyes of the law. The drinkers in The Layman's Arms, however, were only too willing to enter into the spirit of the thing and record their views on the various settlements that have made their way into the media spotlight for a variety of reasons.

Whatever the reason for you picking up this book in the first place, this is when the subject of divorce passes from being an impossible and/or impractical fancy to a considered reality. Whether a husband or a wife, petitioner or respondent, it's not going to be easy but as the man said: forewarned is forearmed and at least you'll know what to expect before that *decree absolute* arrives through the letter box. *The Good Divorce Guide* isn't just about getting through the legal aspects of a divorce; it's also about practical 'forward planning' and putting your life back together afterwards. So even when things seem at their blackest, remember there *is* a life after divorce and it's waiting for you to reach out and take it.

"What we call the beginning is often the end
And to make an end is to make a beginning
The End is where we start from."
[Little Gidding — T S Elliott]

"I give to Elizabeth Parker the sum of £50, whom, through my foolish fondness, I made my wife, and who in return has not spared, most unjustly, to accuse me of every crime regarding human nature, save highway robbery."

Last Will & Testament of Charles Parker,
1785

Chapter One

Knowing the Facts
And Exploring Attitudes

When we've got to the stage where we're seriously considering divorce the last thing we want to think about are fact and figures but there is some comfort in knowing that our situation is *normal.* Although Britain has one of the highest divorce rates in the world, with almost half of all marriages destined to end in the courts, there are still some very negative social attitudes concerning what has become a common, everyday happening for thousands of people.

When the publishers of a short-lived magazine for the divorced and the about-to-be divorced, announced the launch of *Vive* they were instantly accused of encouraging family breakdowns. Other accusations claimed that the magazine was aiming to make divorce more acceptable and permissible and that the publishers were capitalising on family tragedies. But as *Vive's* editor pointed out at the time, they were not setting out to glamorise divorce; they just want to get it out in the open.

Vive was aimed at the growing number of men and women who were about to go through a divorce, or trying to sort out their lives after a long-term relationship, so it was quite surprising to discover that there was obviously still a strong social stigma to the process. This despite the fact that half the adult population had either instigated it, or were on the receiving end of it - not just once but often two or three times. But as the publishers quickly discovered, there might be a lot of it about but it wasn't the done thing to devote an entire magazine to the subject, and it folded in just under a year.

In a recent newspaper article covering the marriage of possibly the two most famous divorced people in the world — Charles and Camilla — journalist Katie Champion remarked that only a decade ago children with divorced parents were the objects of pity. Their families were described as dysfunctional. Today, quite the opposite is true.

"Divorce and remarriage are an essential part of the ordinary fabric of 21st-century life," wrote Champion. "In Britain. 154,000 couples — and rising — formally separate every year. We are all at it, from people in their twenties to those in their sixties ... The nuclear family with 2.4 children is starting to look like a relic."

She goes on: "George Bush Snr once accused the cartoon family *The Simpsons* of being a threat to American family values, but Homer and Marge — still together after many years — now seem incredibly old-fashioned and out of step with the modern world. The most shocking thing about the Osbournes is not that the children have been in and out of rehab and that none of them can utter a sentence without a dozen expletives in it, but that Sharon and Ozzie are still happily married. How quaint. How very last millennium."

STATISTICS

It's estimated that within the next six years, the number of married men and women will fall below 50% of the population, according to Government forecasts published in March 2005.

At present, most of Britain's 42 million adults are married but the Government Actuary's Department predicts that society will change significantly during the next two decades.

By 2011 just 46% of women and 48% of men will be married. By 2031, 46% of men will have never married, against 42% who will be married and 12% widowed or divorced. Nearly 40% of women will have never married, 40% will be married and 21% widowed or divorced.

The number of couples who live together, but who are not married, will almost double to 3.8 million and surprisingly, most are likely to be aged over 45. The number of divorcees will represent about 10% of the adult population for the first time.

These forecasts from the department, whose figures are used to estimate the likely number of households and the costs of the state pension, reveal the extent of the breakdown of the marriage tradition. While the latest figures from the Office for National Statistics show that there were 166,700 divorces in 2003, not to mention the thousands of others who needed to pick up the pieces after the break up of a long term relationship, whether it be gay, lesbian or heterosexual. Of those thousands of couples, 99% of all divorces go through undefended and although 70% of all divorces were awarded to the wife, only just over one fifth were on the grounds of adultery.

We've known for a long time that the highest proportion of divorces are instigated by the wives but suddenly family law is very high on the political agenda and laws are being amended all the time. On a weekly basis, the marital difficulties and settlements of the rich and famous are blazoned across the headlines, with both parties trying to appear 'cool' about the whole thing as another multi-million demand against their personal fortune hits the news complete with details of the other's failings

According to a 2000 report carried out by the consumer information company, Claritas divorce isn't so much about what we've done as where we live. The comparison of divorce rates in 427 towns, came up with the surprising fact that Biggleswade in Bedfordshire was the home of Britain's happiest marriages with only six per cent of the adults divorced or separated.

A spokesman for a local solicitor admitted that the number of divorces handled by the firm had hardly increased over the past 10 years. "It's more of a seasonal thing," she added, "The inquiries come in January and July — after Christmas and the summer holidays when working couples have had to suddenly spend a lot of time together."

Following closely behind were Altrincham, Greater Manchester (6.3%); Beverley in Humberside (6.5%) and Kingswinford in the West Midlands (8.5%). London (22.9%) comes 19th in the list of top 50 towns and cities with the highest divorce and separation.

At the bottom end of the table, the survey showed that in Skelmerdale, Lancashire one in three of the adult population was divorced or separated (32.4% — the country's highest rate). Skelmersdale has high unemployment and spokesmen for the local Citizen's Advice Bureau and Relate, the marriage guidance charity, revealed that a large proportion of the people who consult them have financial problems. Most of the couples are young with children and credit is easy to obtain. Tensions and mutual blame run high when the prospects of wedded bliss fall short and men in particular become stressed if their identity as the provider is undermined.

Highest rate of divorce and separation

Skelmersdale, Lancashire	32.4%
Hove, East Sussex	29.1%
Barking, Essex	26.2%
Southsea, Hampshire	25.9%
Bransholme, Humberside	25.9%
Andover, Hampshire	25.5%
Birkenhead, Merseyside	25.0%
Hastings, East Sussex	25.0%
Wednesbury; West Midlands	25.0%
Wishaw, Stratclyde	24.6%

Lowest rate of divorce or separation

Biggleswade, Bedfordshire	6.0%
Altrincham, Greater Manchester	6.3%
Beverley, Humberside	6.5%
Kingswinford, West Midlands	8.5%
Sevenoaks, Kent	8.6%
Benfleet, Essex	8.6%
Cheshunt, Hertfordshire	8.7%
Sutton Coldfield, West Midlands	9.0%
Pinner, Middlesex	9.1%
Wickford , Essex	9.2%

[The statistics were compiled from 226,000 consumer surveys taken from across Britain.]

In 1999 statistics showed that the annual UK divorce rate had dropped to 160,000 from a recorded 180,000 in 1993, but this apparent reduction masked the fact that there had been a falling number of marriages during that period. It may not be surprising to learn that the financial drain on the public purse is colossal with the annual legal bill for matrimonial and family proceedings calculated at £387 million, a rise of £14 million in four years.

With the average bride and groom destined for the courts in just 10 years - the average age for divorce is 40 for men and 38 for women - with men more likely to remarry than women. Even so, according to the figures from the National Office for Statistics, half of all second marriages will also end in divorce and nearly 60% of third marriages fail.

There we have it — if you're in the position of divorcing you have more in common with the rest of society than you may have previously thought.

WHAT THE EXPERTS SAY

According to the experts, divorce ranks as one of the major stresses in life. It doesn't matter whether you instigate the proceedings or are on the receiving end, it is a lengthy period of immense emotional trauma. There are, we are told, seven recognised stages whereby we run the gauntlet of conflicting emotion but it is unlikely that you and your former partner will progress though these levels at the same speed. One of you may dwell on a particular point for much longer, while the other may sail through that same stage without so much as a blip on the heart-scan of life.

Breakdown

Like dry-rot, the slow disintegration of a marriage can go undetected for months, even years. The growing gulf in common interests, opinion and lifestyle suddenly becomes a chasm with husband and wife on opposite sides of the gap. Can you find a way to bridge the divide, or have things gone too far to be put right? Is someone else involved? Do you *want* to put it right?

Shock

With the realisation that the marriage has, or is about to collapse, panic sets in and reduces us to a lethargic, self-pitying, bewildered mess. No matter how hard we try, the brain simply refuses to function. Men have a tendency to go onto automatic pilot at this stage and carry on as though there's nothing amiss, which gives completely the wrong impression about how they are actually feeling deep down inside and can often be interpreted as being insensitive when they're actually hurting like hell.

Anger

Build up a fine head of steam and smash something. When a friend reached this stage, she kept a box of ill-assorted china and glassware in the garage and whenever the urge came over her, she would go out and hurl a piece at the wall. She always maintained that this kept her a) sane and b) prevented her from doing something *really* stupid and smashing something valuable — belonging to *him*. The display of anger is, of course, the catharsis, or purging of the emotions and the sign that we are beginning to let go of the past. You don't think calming thoughts at this stage — believe me!

Pain

When the anger subsides all we're left with is the dull ache of raw nerve ends. It's probably at this stage when the fact that there's still a flicker of love left in the relationship begins to surface. The sight of family albums or the words from a song playing on Radio 2, can set off a chain reaction of "How can s/he do this to me?" and "How will I manage on my own?"

Hatred

When the pendulum swings back again to loathing and resentment, triggered by the enforced upheaval that resounds to the cry of: "I'll get the bitch/bastard for this!" This often occurs at the low ebb in the proceedings when all the paperwork has finished going backwards and forwards and we feel that any contact is better than none at all. So we harbour visions of revenge. A word of advice ... don't, it will only backfire.

Grief

This usually occurs when the uphill struggles with lawyers, friends, family and spouses are finally put in perspective. There are moments of sad reflection on what might have been if only we'd taken a different stance but there may still be time to salvage some form of friendship from the ashes even if we'd wanted to kill each other at the beginning.

Acceptance
When we know *within ourselves* that it's all over. Don't try to make plans, just take one day at a time and slowly but surely we will strengthen our resolve to make a new start to our life.

Women's responsibility
In *Secrets of Relationship Success*, feisty divorce lawyer, Vanessa Lloyd Platt drew on her 20 years of matrimonial skirmishing to reveal that there has been an alarming increase in the number of men complaining about the conduct of women. Based on personal research and a poll of her own clients, Ms Lloyd Platt has come to the startling conclusion that it is *women's* behaviour that is to blame for Britain's escalating divorce rate and that their men-folk cannot wait to escape from their clutches.

It may appear incongruous that an intelligent, professional woman, wife and mother - and a divorce lawyer to boot - should draw such damning conclusions but the facts are there in black and white. Women may not want to accept that they are responsible for the breakdown of their relationships but the divorce statistics prove this to be the case. In fact, in the majority of divorces, women see themselves as totally blameless, heaping scorn and vitriol on the heads of their ex-partner whenever the opportunity arises regardless of who instigates the action.

Much of the feminist propaganda over the past decade had convinced women that it is possible (and their right) to have a promising career, a stable home life and all the happiness they can handle but Ms Lloyd Platt says "with absolute authority" that without the right kind of attitude, this just *isn't* possible. As a result of the pressures of not being able to cope with a home and a career, the domestic atmosphere resembles the Siberian steppes in deep winter. The career-wife petitions for divorce because her husband (unreasonably) expected her to do *everything*; or he packs his bags and moves out to live with the homely lady from the florist shop.

HOW DID WE GET TO THIS?

Here we need to examine those four reasons for divorcing and decide whether we're hiding behind excuses, or whether we have a justifiable reason for off-loading our partner. A realistic look at why we *really* want a divorce may help to smooth the path towards an amicable settlement without too much blood-letting.

Money:
Cited in song as the root of all evil, it also causes more arguments among established couples than good, old-fashioned sex. Money problems can be the result of too much as well as too little. It can indirectly be linked to resentment over a blossoming career if one partner suddenly starts to earn more than the other, or objects to becoming a corporate husband/wife. Gambling, habitual debt and pilfering from the family pot may be something that cannot be resolved but if the financial 'problem' stems from lack of communication rather than wilful deceit, then there may be time to reverse the breakdown of the relationship.

Sex:
Of course we always have good old-fashioned adultery but sexual differences may be more complicated than the discovery that your partner is having an affair. (Bear in mind that you cannot rely on adultery that you learned about more than six months previously and that the legal definition of adultery is penetrative intercourse between opposite sexes. Oral or 'gay' sex is merely 'unreasonable behaviour'!) Often, it's not until a couple have been married for many years that any sexual differences begin to emerge. For example, one partner may have latent or concealed sexual desires with which the other cannot relate; that the other's sexual demands are intolerable or, that there has been some sexual impropriety. It should be understood that men's and women's attitudes to sex are completely different — what one may see as too often, the other may perceive as not enough. Some women are horrified and humiliated at the discovery of a stock of porn magazine and videos but will quite gleefully go on a hen-night where a live *Full Monty* is the entertainment for the evening!

Intolerable behaviour:
This can range from domestic violence to that wonderfully obtuse legal phrase: irretrievably broken down. Violence and any form of child-abuse, of course, needs no justification but there are subtle and minor irritations that, compounded by years of close proximity, can suddenly implode with devastating results. For example: a man filed for divorce on the grounds of unreasonable behaviour because every day of their married life, his wife had moved the furniture around. After hearing of his years of climbing over and around furniture, the judge ended the 38-year marriage although the wife had contested the divorce. Intolerable behaviour can encompass unsavoury personal habits such as his toenails in the bath, her using his razor, his belching, her farting ... to never wanting to accompany a partner on business occasions, obsessive sports commitments, neglect of the home, or adopting some strange religious belief.

Those who should never have got married in the first place:
Often people from similar backgrounds who mistake companionship for compatibility. The popular couple who sparkle on the motor racing scene and spend nearly every weekend as guests of their married friends find things don't sparkle quite so much when they're harnessed together in a domestic set-up of their own. Conversely, those who start out under the banner of 'opposites attract' can find that their opposing differences leave no common ground for them to share at the end of the day. The sad thing about such cases is that had the couple been content to be 'just good friends' without the misplaced desire to spend the rest of their lives together, they would have had something much more valuable than a failed marriage and its attendant animosity.

Children:
With all the emphasis being placed on the welfare of children affected by divorcing parents, it will probably be considered tantamount to blasphemy to state that children can also be a prime cause for divorce. A study compiled by *Mother & Baby* magazine revealed that having a baby can ruin your sex life, marriage and

career. Partners who have been heavily committed to working and socialising together may find that the arrival of a baby curtails their activities to such a degree that they begin to lead separate lives. The resentment a being left out can manifest itself in many different ways, even if the partner is doing no more than continuing to work as the family breadwinner. Every late evening or business lunch is seen as being out enjoying themselves while the other is left at home to look after the baby. If a couple, or individual, isn't ready for the commitment, it will cause serious difficulties and probably comes under the heading of 'those who shouldn't have got married in the first place'.

Older children can also cause a couple to split up, especially if the child belongs to a former marriage. After four years of happy marriage Beth welcomed her husband's 8-year old son into their home when his mother wanted to emigrate. "Big mistake! It was the playing one off against the other and my husband always believing the boy that caused the problems. As his mother was no longer living in this country there was nowhere for him to go, but by then I couldn't have cared less, so I moved out and left them to it."

WHERE DID IT GO WRONG?
Although financial problems can place a tremendous strain on a relationship, even those with all the advantages find that they can't make it work. Actress Patsy Kensit admitted that she'd cried "every day for three and a half years" while married to rock star Liam Gallagher. In a magazine interview, she insisted that she'd put everything she could into the marriage and that having made a commitment, she was determined to make it successful despite all the warning signs.

Unless the reasons behind wanting a divorce are cut and dried, i.e. sexual transgression or violence, it may not be easy to define why we no longer wish to remain under the same roof as our partner. The following, are some of the reasons that may contribute to the desire to put a lot of miles between ourselves and the person we married. Individually they may not amount to anything significant but compound the pressures over a period of time and any situation can because intolerable. Make a list of these compound issues for both yourself and your partner and see if you can track down where the rot began to set in.

Compound issues relating to career

- resentment of a partner's earnings or reversal of earnings
- resentment of partner's promotion (especially by those in the same profession)
- long hours worked, resulting in missed meals, social invitations, etc
- enforced removal to a new location because of a career move
- not taking a partner's part-time or freelance work seriously
- refusal to take the role of a corporate husband or wife
- ridicule should a partner attempt to 'better themselves' through education
- the belief that one partner is socially inadequate (i.e. holding the other back)

Compound issues relating to money

- desire for financial independence
- one partner taking complete control of financial matters
- not making any financial contribution to the domestic finances
- parsimony and penny-pinching
- profligacy and extravagance
- running up debts on credit or store cards
- concealing debts
- gambling

Compound issues relating to children

- partner changes their mind about wanting children
- pressure brought bear to have a pregnancy terminated
- arguments over children's education
- one partner directs all their attention/affection onto the children
- refusal to accept an invitation if children are not included
- step-children cause problems between parent and new spouse

- resentment between step-children and children of new marriage
- excessive maintenance payments to children of previous marriage

Compound issues relating to retirement, redundancy or bankruptcy

- having a partner at home all day and disrupting the domestic routine
- lack of sympathy/understanding of the stress caused by change of circumstances
- resentment over the down-grading of lifestyle
- made to feel like a has-been or failure
- lack of finances for holidays, social events, etc.
- social stigma
- resentment at having to start over again
- necessity to move away from friends, family, etc.

Compound issues relating to age

- realisation that 'there's not a lot of time left for things to happen'
- realising the need to 'discover yourself'
- your partner has aged much faster than you and doesn't want to do anything
- your partner has aged less than you and still wants to be out and about
- making the break now the children have left home
- conflicting religious interests
- nothing in common
- financial insecurity

Compound issues relating to health

- resentment of a partner's disability or illness
- unable to cope with a partner's disability or illness
- intolerance of 'self-inflicted' problems such as alcohol or drug abuse

- unable to cope with or tolerate psychological problems
- no longer willing to pander to a hypochondriac
- belief that you would not properly cared for in the case of illness
- financial insecurity
- conflicting dietary preferences

Compound issues relating to sex
- discovering that your partner is having an affair
- unwilling to remain married to a serial adulterer
- partner's sexual desires are incompatible
- partner's sexual preferences are incompatible
- objection to partner's penchant for pornography
- you no longer find your partner sexually attractive
- you have the need for outside sexual adventures
- conflicting religious beliefs concerning sexual matters

Compound issues relating to behaviour
- verbal or physical violence
- unfounded jealousy (over friends, family, pets, etc.)
- psychological or mental cruelty
- unwilling to remain with a 'control freak'
- objection to offensive personal hygiene or habits
- lack of conversation or communication
- the need for companionship
- inconsiderate and/or selfish behaviour

Surprisingly enough, very few of the above 'compound issues' relate to sex and yet most people are probably under the impression that most marriage failures are due to adulterous behaviour. This is far from a comprehensive list - but you have to stop somewhere. Try making a 'His' and 'Hers' listing and, being as honest as you can, list who's committed which offences. Odds are that it will be about 50/50 — if you're honest that is!

BEING OPEN AND HONEST

Not the easiest thing to be under the present circumstances. Unless the divorce has been exacerbated by violence or sex misdemeanour, it's odds on that under close examination your reasons in the cold light of day could appear trite and petty. If you're going to come through this relatively unscathed at the end of all the skirmishing, it's time to admit (even if it's only to yourself) that the breakdown of your relationship is pretty even-sided.

Unfortunately, people tend to shy away from self-analysis for the simple reason that they don't want to look at the image staring back at themselves.

When Debbie decided to divorce Dave for his 'unreasonable behaviour' it took her a long time to admit to herself that she was embarrassed to be married to a "squalid little grease-monkey with a back street garage". The reason for her self-perceived elevation of her own status was her new membership to the local sports and health club, that Dave had given her for her birthday. Playing tennis and badminton with what she saw as classier people made her feel she was entitled to a better life-style.

A man of few words, Dave was hurt over her attack on what he saw as his efforts to give her a nice life-style but he didn't contest the divorce. He did warn her that there wasn't any money as the garage was mortgaged to the hilt; he also tried to point out that her new-found friends at the health club would dump her once was single again. He was subsequently proved to be correct which has caused Debbie to writhe with animosity towards him since the health-club members whose business she solicited on his behalf, continue to use the garage. He has since met someone else and is now learning to play squash at the same club as his former wife.

TAKING THE FIRST STEPS

Before making any public declaration about your intentions, it would be a good idea to provide yourself with some facts and figures about the property, savings or any other capital that the court will need to take into account in the event of divorce. Bear in mind that this may also include any inheritances, compensation received for personal injuries or redundancy pay.

Checklist:

1. What property do each of you own in your own name — houses, furniture and other contents, land, stock, shares, pension policies, life insurances, investments, cash in banks, building societies or in other accounts.
2. If either of you are self-employed a certain proportion of your savings will in due course be payable to the Inland Revenue and should be deducted from the total. What is the value of that tax liability?
3. What property do you own in joint names with your spouse or anyone else?
4. Did either of you own any property before you were married or acquire it after you were separated? Did any of it come by way of gift or inheritance from your families? If so, what property comes in these categories?
5. What are the current values of all the property involved? Will costs or duties be payable if any of it is sold and, if so, what is its value of any costs?
6. What mortgages exist in your name, your partner's or jointly, and how much is outstanding on them. Have payments due on mortgages or agreements been maintained and, if not, what arrears are outstanding?
7. Are any balances outstanding on hire, hire purchase and credit cards, joint or separate?
8. What debts do you or your partner have, joint or separate?
9. Are current accounts for public utility services — electricity, gas, telephone — in the name of the person who is using the service and who will continue to receive the bills and be liable for them unless or until the supplier is informed otherwise?
10. If any transfer of property is involved, will the date or manner of the transfer mean that the liability of taxes or any other duty will arise? If not, what will it cost?

Establishing the facts

Regardless of which side of the divorce petition you are, ideally, you need to establish exactly what each of you has, what it is worth, what your liabilities will be if it is sold and what your debts are. You should also take steps to preserve the property intact until a legal financial settlement has been reached and stamped by the court. The following steps may help:

• If you own property (a house or bank account) in joint names, is it held on terms which will result in your joint owner acquiring the lot automatically if you die unexpectedly? It may be wise for you to serve a notice ending the joint tenancy immediately so that your share will pass to your estate, in the event of your death before the divorce is finalised. Should you arrange for the bank to freeze any joint account, or open a new one for your personal use?

• Is there any property in the name of your husband or wife alone? Have you done anything to prevent them disposing of it or mortgaging it without your approval before a legal agreement can be settled?

• Until your marriage is actually dissolved by *decree absolute*, your husband or wife will have the same rights under your will as he or she would have had if you were still living happily together. Should you change your will, if you have not already done so?

THE WARRING FACTIONS

Once the intention to divorce is brought out into the open, family and friends quickly declare under which colours they will be enjoined in battle. Everyone wants a chance at 'plain speaking' and will encourage you to 'get the bitch/bastard' and take them for everything they've got. It is quite frightening just how high feelings can run when you are forced to listen to the slanderous attack made against the man or woman you've been living with for the past decade in blissful ignorance of outside opinion.

The legal profession always maintains that a solicitor will always act in the best interests of their client and that there is no point in seeking expert advice and then ignoring it. True, but there are also numerous occasions where the couple were divorcing quite amicably until a solicitor put an oar in and turned the whole negotiating process upside down.

"Tony and I had already sorted out between us who was to get what from the house, when one of the solicitors started moving the goalposts," said Sandra. "Letters started going backwards and forwards, adopting an increasingly belligerent tone until we'd fallen out completely. After weeks of non-cooperation, Tony and I met up for lunch and renegotiated our terms on two paper napkins. These were handed to our respective solicitors who were told to get on with it. Yes, I was entitled to a higher cash settlement but I preferred to keep the friendship which has now endured for ten years since our divorce."

It is important that neither of you become over-reliant upon your solicitor when it comes to communication. The two people best able to sort out any difficulties are you and your partner and providing you can bite your tongue when s/he starts to irritate you, things may just work out fine in the end.

"The problem is that family and friends don't want you to remain on good terms with your ex," admitted Jack. "I found being on the receiving end of the divorce extremely hurtful but in the end I had to accept that Pam wanted out and that my unpleasantness wasn't going to change anything. My family are horrified that I can still meet her for lunch and enjoy her company. *They* can't handle it. We're fine."

CONSIDERING RELIGIOUS DIFFICULTIES

If you or your partner comes from an orthodox religious background, there may be the additional complication of your divorce being at odds with the tenets of your faith. Whatever anyone may tell you, there is nothing that can stop you applying for a Judicial Separation - a court order confirming that the parties are legally separated - as an alternative to divorce. This is often used in cases where religious reasons prevent a divorce but you should consult a lawyer who understands the implications and if you're unsure about who you can talk to, have a quiet word with the local Citizen's Advice Bureau.

In many cases, it may be necessary for you to accept that whatever the reason behind your seeking a divorce, it may not be recognised by your religious leaders. Whatever you do, you will be in a no-win situation and so you'll need to summon the extra strength to deal with disapproving relatives *and* community, in addition to the trauma of the divorce itself. If your family refuses its support then it may be necessary to decide on taking more drastic measures, and if you are positive that this *is* the right move to make, then you should let no-one stand in your way. But make sure you are in possession of all the facts before showing your hand.

Dissidence

It is not uncommon for people to take umbrage when a 'priest' refuses to condone certain behaviour in which we wish to participate, but which goes against the teaching of that particular religious establishment. Here we find potential divorcees believing they have the right to flout the rules without censor and yet still remain part of a formal religious grouping.

For example, the Roman Catholic Church's stance on divorce is quite clear and 'loyal' Roman Catholics are duty bound to accept the directive without question. Here we cannot 'maintain the right to propagate opinions contrary to the teaching authority of the Church' whilst demanding the right to be classed as a staunch member of that establishment. One is either a 'Roman' Catholic or a dissident catholic and those bending the rules on divorce are, in fact, dissidents.

Although every priest is bound to uphold the religious laws of their faith, one rabbi took the unprecedented step of 'naming and shaming' a man in the *Jewish Chronicle*. The former husband had refused his wife a *get* (a religious divorce), despite the fact that their marriage had ended in 1991. Without a *get,* the divorced wife was prevented from remarrying in a synagogue and neither could the children of the second marriage be bought up as orthodox Jews.

Coping with personal prejudice

There are times, however, when a priest will decide to take a moral stance that does not necessarily reflect the over-view of the religious establishment. Such as the village rector who offended marriage counselling groups by maintaining that divorcing couples should be investigated by the courts for "mental and spiritual child abuse". He believed that couples should stay together and "suffer" for the sake of the children. He claimed in the church newsletter that children could cope with drunkenness and domestic violence but divorce resulted in them failing at school and turning to drugs and crime.

Should you find yourself in the position of having to cope with someone's *personal* prejudices that are not part of official religious doctrine, then it's obviously time to find a place where it isn't necessary to stand in the presence of such rugged grandeur. It is a serious issue for all families contemplating divorce and a spokes-man for the bishopric was quick to comment that to accuse *all* divorcing parents of mental and spiritual abuse of their children clearly lacked compassion and understanding. The answer is simple: take your custom elsewhere.

On the opposite side of the religious divide and one of the more frightening aspects of religious differences is the situation where one parent uses the other's pagan beliefs as grounds for them not being considered a fit parent. This is *not* an isolated problem, and although divorce among pagans is far below the national average, the accusations usually come from the child's absent parent and/or grand-parents who try everything they can to undermine the mother's (or, in some cases, father's) right to become 'parent with care'.

Many lawyers are not aware that a precedent was set by Judge Wooley when he found in favour of the pagan father whose wife, originally a professed pagan herself, left him but did not claim custody of their son. When she later filed for custody, she cited her ex-husband's beliefs as making him unsuitable to bring up the child. This was a long, drawn-out case during which the validity of pagan belief was put under the legal spotlight for the first time but, after many hours of intensive questioning, Judge Wooley granted the father custody of his son.

WHEN ALL ELSE FAILS

It is highly likely that you're not reading this book because you've made up your mind to go for a divorce. If that were the case you'd be talking to a solicitor, not sitting there considering your options. You are probably reading this book because you are confused, resentful or angry about your marriage. But you won't be alone ...

The London law firm of Mishcon de Reya, who handled the divorce of Diana, Princess of Wales conducted a survey which revealed that nearly a quarter of divorces consider leaving their partner within the first two years of marriage. And despite couples' dread of partners succumbing to the 'seven-year itch', a third of divorcees had filed for divorce before their fifth wedding anniversary.

More than a quarter (27%) of divorcees said that their 'sexless' marriages pulled them apart, while one in 10 said their spouse's family had been a contributing factor. A spokesman for the law firm said: "People start to think about divorce many years before they actually get divorced. Couples should have clearer expectations and frank discussions about where they are going."

According to Relate, the marriage counselling service: "Men are simply too lazy to get divorced, and often it is the woman feeling the most hurt and upset about what is going on, so she takes charge of the situation herself. The effect of women with children working full or part-time also has a significant impact. There is a lot of stress coming home because there is not enough time to do things."

The divorce trend analyst Dr Patrick Dixon, author of the book, *The Rising Price of Love*, said: "It's the women who usually have custody of the children, which is why there is a significant difference between the willingness of men and women to break up.

So, you may be the one who is initiating the proceedings; or maybe you've just received your partner's petition and feel that you've drifted into uncharted waters. Should the latter be the case, then you have also got to cope with the reality that your partner has been planning this for some time. For both of you, when all else has failed, divorce *is* the only solution.

There's no great mystery surrounding the divorce process — it is merely a legal device for dissolving the state of marriage. Neither is there any real significance over who instigates the proceedings and what reason they give. As family practice lawyer commented: "Although the current law still demands someone to be at fault, there is no financial penalty attached to the 'guilty' party unless, of course, the behaviour is so outrageous that it cannot be ignored. It just causes added difficulties if the petitioner tries to take a moral high-ground just to put themselves in a favourable light."

CAN WE TAKE CONTROL

There's a Japanese maxim that says *'Don't waste time apportioning blame; identify the problem and solve it'.* Of course, you can't make someone talk if they've made up their mind not to, but regardless of which side you're on, it's essential that you keep the divorce in perspective if your going to take control of *your* affairs and minimise the upheaval.

Taking control doesn't mean directing operations and riding rough shod over anything your partner says or does; it means having a clear idea of where you're heading in the aftermath of divorce. Privately, you might be glad and thankful to see the back of him/her but it doesn't solve anything if you persist in making these views public. Try to put as much distance between you as possible without being 'unavailable' since there's always the urge to have the last word — even (or especially), if it's going to cause a row.

Pay attention to the divorces that make the headlines in the newspapers and ask yourself whether you want to come out looking like the *heartless bastard v. calculating bitch* of the tabloid headlines. Taking control means walking away with dignity and self-respect intact regardless of what your ex- is saying to justify his/her reasons for filing for divorce. On the other hand, if you've managed to prevent yourself from apportioning blame, it might be that there's still time to identify the problems that have arisen between you and take the opportunity to try to solve them. Even if the only outcome is a civilised divorce.

VIEWPOINTS FROM THE LAYMAN'S ARMS
In true bar-room lawyer style, the opinions given in the Layman's Arms sections are based on publicised case histories, newspaper reports and gossip, not actual court transcripts; they nevertheless reflect the view of the man and woman at the bar.

Although his wife was acquitted of attempting to murder her multimillionaire husband by drugging him before trying to suffocate him with a plastic bag, he was 'stunned' by the jury's verdict. She claimed she only intended to shock him; he seriously thought she meant to kill him.

According to the husband, she'd ordered him to destroy his late wife's letters and photographs. She'd also taken to wearing his late wife's clothes and adopted a heavy-handed approach to his three daughters who were still coming to terms with their mother's death from cancer two years earlier.

No doubt the 18-month marriage will still cost him a pretty penny following the subsequent divorce proceedings but from a moral point of view, should he really be expected to pay anything?

Male opinion:
"This woman should consider herself lucky that she's not behind bars. She shouldn't be entitled to anything in terms of a divorce settlement. The husband was and still is clearly disturbed by his first wife's death, and his new wife made a point of trying to make him feel much worse by wearing his firs wife's clothes, something which was undoubtedly intended to unsettle him further.

Her heavy-handed approach towards the children shows she was not a caring, loving person but someone was only out to get what she wanted. Claiming that she only meant to shock him by drugging him and attempting to suffocate him with a plastic bag simply doesn't wash. Perhaps the jury could not be absolutely certain that murder was intended and by some incredible stroke of luck she was acquitted. She ought to be awarded 1p in settlement and nothing more."

"I think not. This woman plainly married him for his money, so no money should be given. An example should be set in this case."

Female opinion:
"From a practical point of view, I know he is going to be stung for this marriage, and he will just have to put it down to experience. He didn't know the woman very well before he married her and getting your leg over for a couple of weeks is no basis for a lasting marriage (not to mention endangering your finances and your children's well-being). From a moral point of view, I think it really takes the biscuit that, after her trying to murder him and failing, he will no doubt have to pay for the privilege of getting shot of her. I think she ought to be paying him damages!"

"Perhaps a *small* settlement but she sounds an insecure, manipulative person who should have known that neither the man nor his family were over their grief. He was lonely—she was desperate."

"The trouble is, Jane is still young enough to think one man may be better than another."

Jennie Lee, *The Times*—writing about a friend's divorce

Chapter Two

Finding a Lawyer

According to the Office for National Statistics, the number of people getting divorced reached its highest level for seven years in the summer of 2003, with the highest rate of marital breakdown involving women under 30, with couples splitting up earlier. The highest number of marriage breakdowns occurred between men aged 30-34 and women aged 25-29, or where there had been a premarital conception. The survey showed that there were an increasing number of divorces among people on their second or even third marriage, with the average age at divorce rising slightly to 41.9 and 39.4 for men and women, with a marriage lasting about 11 years.

In most cases, however, by the time those seeking a divorce get around to consulting a solicitor someone will have done or said something silly which escalates the problem from disagreement to antagonism and unwise actions. There is no law that stipulates a private individual must have a solicitor but the law can often be complex and uncertain, especially in times of stress and emotional upheaval. Legal procedures are not always a matter of common sense and the law is famed for throwing more than its fair share of curved balls at the wicket.

Added to this, as barrister Laurence Kingsley observes in *You & Your Solicitor:* "The mere mention of a solicitor can provoke conflicting emotions in even the most balanced of people. Solicitors are often feared and disliked by their clients as they are revered and obeyed by them. As a body, solicitors are despised, joked about and may be the least popular of all professions."

This, coupled with the fact that their fees are looked upon as 'money for old rope', with costs often running into thousands of pounds, it is not really surprising that we fight shy of consulting a solicitor when we're at our most vulnerable. With the fear of costs mounting with each phone call and letter, it is understandable why so many people take the wrong action for the right reasons, or the right action for the wrong ones. So what *are* the options?

MAKING DECISIONS

In an ideal world, where a couple can reach an amicable settlement, without complication or argument, it can take as little as three months to obtain a divorce. In England and Wales they would be eligible to divorce if they have been:

a. married for at least a year;
b. domiciled in England or Wales, or have been habitually resident there for at least one year; and
c. able to *prove* that the marriage had irretrievably broken down.

In order to provide such proof, the Petitioner (the person who starts the divorce proceedings) must be able to demonstrate that the Respondent (the person on whom the petition is to be served) has:

- Committed adultery and that the Petitioner finds it intolerable to live with him/her: adultery.
- Or the Respondent has behaved in such a way that the parties cannot reasonably be expected to go on living together: unreasonable behaviour.
- Or the Respondent has deserted the Petitioner for a continuous period of at least two years: desertion.
- Or the Petitioner and the Respondent have lived apart for a continuous period of at least two years and the Respondent agrees to the divorce: two years separation by consent.
- Or the Petitioner and the Respondent have lived apart for a continuous period of at least five years: five years separation. The Respondent does not have to consent to the divorce in this case.

If all is plain sailing, it is possible to petition for a divorce under the 'Special Procedure' through the county court if you live in England or Wales. For those living in Scotland, Northern Ireland and Eire, however, the process can differ quite considerably and it is advisable to contact the Law Society for referral to a specialist family law practitioner.

THE 'SPECIAL PROCEDURE'

In England and Wales you can start divorce proceedings in any County Court (or at the Principal Registry in London), which are listed in the telephone directory under 'Courts'. To get the ball rolling you will need to apply for a 'Divorce Petition' form and if children are involved, a 'Statement of Arrangements for Children' form, both of which are supplied free of charge by the County Court.

Once the divorce petition has been completed, it should be sent back to the country court, together with the following documents:

- A copy of the divorce petition for the Respondent. If a third party is being named as co-respondent in the case of adultery, then a third copy should be attached.)

- The original marriage certificate or a certified copy — photocopies are not acceptable.

- The required fee (unless your financial circumstances render you exempt).

- If there are children involved, the completed 'Statement of Arrangement' form, together with a copy for the Respondent.

- If you are being advised by a solicitor, and not eligible for Community Legal Service Funding (formerly Legal Aid), your solicitor must submit a Certificate of Reconciliation to confirm that the possibility of reconciling the marriage has been discussed.

Providing all the paperwork is in order, the court will serve the petition on the Respondent, together with an 'Acknowledgement of

Service' form that acts as a confirmation that the petition has been received. It also asks the Respondent whether they intend to contest the proceedings; whether they object to a claim for costs; and whether they wish to make their own application for an order concerning any children of the marriage. The Respondent has eight days from receipt of the 'Acknowledgement of Service' to complete and return it to the court, together with a written statement if there is any disagreement over the content of the 'Statement of Arrangements'. It's important to keep all the paperwork together to avoid any of the documents going missing and resulting in delay while they are located.

Issuing the decrees

Once the court has received the Respondent's completed 'Acknowledgement of Service' form, a copy is sent to the Petitioner together with a blank affidavit that asks for confirmation of the accuracy of the contents of the petition. The court registrar will then consider the forms and, if they are in order, will give directions for the case to be entered into the Special Procedure list. If there is no objection to the *decree nisi*, it will then be granted automatically. No one need attend the court hearing unless they wish to object. (If there is any dispute about the children, or if for any reason the judge is not satisfied with the arrangements proposed for them, he will adjourn the case, possibly for a full court hearing if the disputes cannot be resolved.) The judge confirms the *decree nisi* and the court office will then send a copy to both parties.

A *decree nisi* is only a provision measure and does not end the marriage, neither does it alter the fact that you are still husband and wife in law. Six weeks and one day after the *decree nisi* has been granted, application must be made to the court for this to be made into a *decree absolute.* Unless cause is shown why it should not take effect, or if there are no conditions attached to nullify the decree, the *degree absolute* is then a formality, once the fee of £30 has been paid. If, after three months the Petitioner has not made application, the Respondent can apply for a *decree absolute* instead. The court registrar will then send copies to both parties and the marriage is legally over.

WHEN A DISPUTE ARISES

If, when we thought that everything was moving along quite nicely, our ex- decides to throw a spanner in the works by refusing to comply with what we thought was a firm agreement, there are three important things we must do:

- Don't panic

- Consult your solicitor immediately

- Resist the urge to retaliate

Panic is a natural reaction because we feel hurt and betrayed by someone on whom we'd placed our trust, even though the relationship was over. "And I believed the bitch/bastard," is an often repeated refrain following the reneging of a private agreement, hotly pursued by "What am I going to do now?"

You must consult a solicitor if you haven't already and nip any long, drawn-out haggling in the bud. Here you should be realistic about *why* there's been a change to the agreed course of action. Hurt, confusion or relief may have been the reason why our partner made the agreement in the first place but on reflection may now have considered themselves brain-dead to have given in so completely. This change of heart may have been at the instigation of a solicitor, the girls in the office, or even his/her mother! The most important thing is to seek some form of dialogue before things get out of hand.

Although it may be difficult, you must resist the urge to retaliate and try to get to grips with the reasons behind the change of mind. Perhaps the agreement *was* unfair. The courts don't apportion blame for a break-up so we can't expect any preferential treatment when splitting assets even if you are the innocent party. Were you relying on a guilt trip to obtain a better deal by making your ex- feel bad?

Whatever the reasons, this is not the time for histrionics, so let the solicitor find out what went wrong, and why?

MEDIATION AND 'FAIR WITNESS'

Unfortunately, life is not always simple and divorces tend to drag on because neither party will give in to the other's demands. It is in both your interests to consult a solicitor *before* the divorce proceedings start as they will be able to offer advice and the necessary information that will protect you and your financial interests, both during the proceedings and after the marriage has been declared legally over.

Problems usually arise once the Respondent has seen the Petitioner's demands (and reasons for wanting a divorce) set down in black and white. As solicitor David Green wrote in *Splitting Up,* even if they were "right-thinking persons before they received their petitions, they ceased to be afterwards — unless a draft of the terms of the petition has already been made known to them beforehand and has been tacitly agreed to facilitate a swift and harmonious divorce".

Using mediation

So how can you facilitate this harmonious state of affairs without the other party rearing up on their hind legs and trading punches on the steps of the court house? The answer is often mediation — a process introduced in 1997 that offers both parties the opportunity to come to an agreement that satisfies them both. When we take into account that solicitor's fees can cost anything between £70 and £200 per hour (not to mention the additional 'disbursements') and that a legal bill in excess of £3,500 is considered normal, then there must be a better way. Bear in mind that the more the legal costs, the less there will be to help us put our lives in order afterwards.

Mediation is often misunderstood to mean marriage guidance counselling, so perhaps a better term would be 'fair witness'. A mediator is a neutral and impartial 'fair witness', whose job is not to advise but to help a couple reach agreement by negotiation. The process doesn't, of course, suit everyone but with an impartial third party acting a 'piggy in the middle' there is more than a slim chance we can reach an amicable solution without killing each other over something trivial that's been allowed to blow up out of all proportion.

Unlike marriage guidance, which sets out to resolve a couple's differences in an attempt to reunite them, or reconcile them to separation, mediation assumes that the relationship is already over. It is simply a means of reaching agreement about practical matters — access to the children, money, property — without the considerable stress and expense of going to court. As dissatisfaction with the family law courts grows — high-lighted in particular by the pressure group Fathers 4 Justice — mediation is becoming more and more popular.

Mediation is provided by a number of recognised professional organisations, so check their procedure before making an appointment. In most cases the Petitioner and the Respondent do not discuss their circumstances in front of each other; the mediator obtains all the necessary information during individual sessions and then offers suggestions to each of them in separate interviews often over eight to ten meetings each.

Advantages of mediation

Negotiations are carried out face to face without the involvement of solicitors and if you can manage to behave like sensible human beings, you can sign a legally-binding Deed of Separation covering every area of interest without a single solicitor having to fire a warning shot across anyone's bows. Needless to say, this outcome is dependent upon you being able to discuss your own future plans, finances and worries about the children without things degenerating into a full scale row, since you no longer have to discuss things with each other.

An even greater advantage is that mediation encourages people to retain control over their lives and, what is even *more* important, their self-respect and dignity. Having someone who is non-judgemental helps us to remain focussed on the *practical* issues of divorce rather than descending into recrimination and self-pity, especially where access to children is concerned. Mediation lessens the cost of divorce quite considerably, and the fees depend on the extent of the problem surrounding the settlement and the number of sessions required to resolve it.

Disadvantages of mediation

In the early days, many solicitors, weren't convinced that mediation was the answer. One family law solicitor maintained that it can only work when the couple involved are of "equal standing, emotionally, intellectually and practically and when the decision to divorce is mutually acceptable". As the lawyer rightly points out, it is *very* rare that a couple reach a mutually amicable decision to split.

In the early days, research concluded by the Family Law Mediation Pilot Project reported that of the 3,000 people a month attending the initial meetings, only 20% (some 7-8,000 a year) actually go through the whole process of mediation. This contrasts dramatically with the Family Dispute Resolution hearings that were introduced into the legal system for handling divorce cases in June 2000. These hearings gave the couple, together with their solicitors, the opportunity to discuss all the issues involved in the case in a close court, with the view to the judge giving an opinion on how it is likely to progress. The aim being to encourage both parties to reach an agreed settlement, rather than having one imposed by the court.

By 2003, there were 260 publicly funded mediation services across England and Wales, and in the previous year 13,841 meditations were started: more than double the figure for 1999/2000. It is a service now offered by most legal firms (largely solicitors, but some barristers), private companies and not-for-profit organisations or charities staffed by solicitors, therapists and counsellors, so the initial misgivings appear to have largely evaporated.

Could mediation help?

Many couples can't talk to each other but find it easier to discuss things with a stranger, especially if one partner has a volatile nature that the other finds intimidating. Others will resent what they see as interference and prefer the detached professionalism of a solicitor to negotiate on their behalf

Ask yourself the following questions:

- Would I be willing to discuss my financial position with a mediator?

- Would my ex- be willing to discuss his/her financial affairs with a mediator?

- How far am I prepared to compromise in order to obtain a sensible settlement?

- Would my ex- be open to compromise?

- How reasonable am I prepared to be over contact with the children?

- Are there any reasons why I should object to my ex's contact with the children?

Mediation and/or Family Dispute Resolution hearings will become increasingly more and more in the spotlight as the 'powers that be' try to cut the mounting costs of Community Legal Service Funding (formerly Legal Aid) since divorce cases cost the taxpayer £15+ billion a year. It's highly probable that in a few years time, we will see the law changed to automatically incorporate some form of mediation into the divorce petition but in the meantime, a voluntary decision to avail ourselves of the service, might improve the quality of life when it's all over.

And if your ex- is still reluctant, or refuses point-blank to see a mediator, just point out that the potential £7,000 legal bill will come out of his or her share of the settlement.

FINDING THE RIGHT (WO)MAN FOR THE JOB

Choosing the right solicitor isn't always easy although most practices will allow us half an hour of free advice which gives us the opportunity to see whether we are happy with this person acting on our behalf. But initial appearances can be deceptive.

"The first solicitor I saw struck me as being brisk, sharp and efficient; throughout the first interview she exuded competent and professionalism," said Mandy. "As things progressed, however, there was a definite air of 'Let's get the bastard' which I found unsettling. I only wanted what was rightfully mine not get tangled up in a crusade for women's rights. In the end I went to another solicitor who looked like somebody's granddad. The fact that he had a mind like a steel trap meant my husband wasn't allowed to get away with anything but at least there was no undercurrent or hidden agenda."

So how do you find the right solicitor? Where possible, personal recommendations from those who have gone before are likely to be the most acceptable. Do bear in mind that the family lawyers who have been involved with both parties over the years will usually decline act for you on the grounds that they cannot act fairly for either against the other. They will, of course, have established contacts with other practices and will also be in the position to give a personal recommendation. If on the other hand, you have never been in the position before of having to consult a solicitor, then the Citizen's Advice Bureau is a good place to start.

With still over 140,000 divorces a year coming to court, not to mention the thousands of couples separating after a long-term relationship, it is obvious that 'family law work' is the bread and butter of the legal profession. Most law firms have one or more solicitors who specialise in divorce and its related problems. "Do not imagine," writes David Green (*Splitting Up*), "that there is some select band of experts, hidden away, whose skills are so overpowering that they are likely to make any profound difference to the outcome of your case."

This myth of the 'super lawyer' is generated by the celebrity divorces that are never out of the headlines and which throw telephone numbers around in place of settlement figures. In reality, the chances are that we will be reasonably served by any firm of solicitors who are prepared to act on our behalf. If the ideal solicitor still evades us, we can always consult the Solicitors Family Law

Association or Family Lawyers via the Law Society for details of their members in our locality. Remember that Family Lawyers:

- have heard it all before;
- are not going to sit in judgement, regardless of whether you're the Plaintive or the Respondent;
- will be more concerned about the provision for the children than your track record as a serial adulterer;
- will not be intimidated by ranting and bluster;
- will advise you not to comply with demands that are not in your best interest;
- ensure that there are no unresolved financial matters that can be re-opened at a later date

Solicitors are normal human beings like everyone else and, as with life in general, there will be the odd character with whom we feel uncomfortable. Like Mandy, we may object to the attitude/ approach but if your case is straightforward, it may only be necessary to see the solicitor for a couple of appointments, so does it matter that you don't want to spend the rest of your life with him or her?

TALKING IT OVER WITH A LAWYER

In many cases, it will be necessary to discuss some of the most intimate details concerning your marriage - and this can mean talking openly and honestly about things that you wouldn't normally tell your priest, best friend or mother. If the reasons for wanting a divorce are relating to some form of sexual transgression, then your solicitor *will* need to know all about it. Of course it's extremely embarrassing to discuss such topics with a comparative stranger but to echo the words immortalised in *Dragnet:* "G'me the fact, m'am (or sir). Just the facts."

To avoid having to dredge up the details in the cold light of day, when things sound either trite and hollow, or histrionic and drama-laden, write everything down in the correct chronological order, especially if it involves allegations of your partner's unreasonable behaviour. Begin with details of the people involved (in the case of adultery it isn't necessary to name the person with whom your partner has committed adultery if you don't want to) — full names, addresses and dates of birth of all the adults and children, together with marriage and birth certificates. Give the date (or approximate dates) of all the specific instances/examples that have a direct bearing in an exact sequence of events.

Prepare a complete financial statement showing your income and the sources, including details of tax, National Insurance contributions, pensions, mortgage interests and listing all other deductions which come out of it. Where possible, attach a statement of income certified by your employer or the Inspector of Taxes and copies of your accounts for the previous three-year period if you are self-employed. List any details of property you own, either singly or jointly and of all mortgages and debts. If you can provide full details as listed in Chapter One, all well and good.

Unless your solicitor specifically requests any further details, don't clutter up the meeting with superfluous information. Now, however, is a good time to mention:

- several itemised family heirlooms to be allocated as your share of the assets;

- any valuable items that your ex- is likely to remove from the family home;

- if your ex- may resort to violence against you or damage joint assets

If your solicitor requests additional information, provide as quickly a possible and resist the urge to communicate by telephone. By preparing this information well in advance could save you at least a couple of hours in solicitor's fees

HOW MUCH WILL IT COST?

How long is a piece of string? It is extremely difficult, if not impossible to calculate how much the legal fees will amount to in a divorce case and the final bill will depend on the work your solicitor needs to do and the time it takes to do it. Needless to say, cost is an important consideration and a solicitor is obliged to give some idea of the costs he is likely to charge. Apart from fixed court fees and expenses, the only cost a solicitor can reasonably quote in advance will reflect the hourly rates charged for the different levels of legal qualification. Fees are usually calculated by the time of the person actually doing the work — partners will cost more than assistant solicitors, legal executives or articled clerks.

Unless you have Community Legal Service Funding (Legal Aid), your solicitor will probably request an advance payment on account of the costs, and he may also invoice you periodically as the work progresses. Be warned: he is not under any obligation to continue to act for you if you do not comply with any previously agreed financial arrangements.

Community Funding

There are now several different categories of Community Funding and you may be eligible for help with solicitors' fees if you only have a modest disposable income. If there are children involved you may be able to apply for General Family Help to cover the costs of resolving what is considered to be a family dispute. *Note: All forms of Community Funding are now treated as a form of loan that must be repaid once the divorce has been granted.* Those is receipt of Community Funding are allowed to retain around £2,500 worth of assets and if the settlement received from the marriage is high enough, you will be required to pay back the full amount of the loan.

In many areas of England and Wales, Community Funding has only be granted if an initial meeting with a mediator has been attended to discuss the possibility of taking this road rather than formal hand to hand combat via a solicitor. Eligibility for free mediation is means-tested but should it be granted, it is not treated as a loan, and neither is the solicitor who will act for you in drawing up legal agreements or consent orders once the mediation is completed.

The pilot study, however, revealed that people weren't willing to accept mediation when they were forced into it and, as a result, demanded 'proper legal advice' from lawyers instead. In Scotland, it is still possible to obtain legal aid and all mediators are experienced, practising family lawyers if you go through the Comprehensive Accredited Lawyer Mediator scheme.

Chalking up the costs

Even a 'simple' legal dispute between a couple that cannot agree a settlement over the children and the marital home, can quickly chalk up costs of £6,000+ on both sides. And the longer the dispute goes on (with solicitor's fees averaging £100 an hour) the less capital each will have to start again. If one party works full-time (i.e. the husband), the whole of the £6,000 cost must be paid immediately, regardless of whether the family home is to be sold now or later.

With children involved, a court will acknowledge the husband's right to a share of the proceeds but he may not be able to collect until his children cease full-time education — which could be several years in the future if the court defers the sale. If the other half of the couple (i.e. the wife) requires the services of Community Funding then, of the £6,000 costs, the wife would still have to pay £3,500 when the property was eventually sold.

If our mythical couple had opted for mediation (and it had been successful) then the husband's costs would have amounted to around £700 while the wife would have had to pay nothing at all.

BEING ON THE RECEIVING END

It takes two to bring about a divorce but what happens if we are the one who is reluctant (for whatever reason) for this to go ahead. Even if we've agreed to the separation, it can be extremely hurtful to receive a copy of a divorce petition that is nothing less than a character assassination by someone with whom we've shared our life for the past ten years.

When the Petitioner casts his/her mind back over the marriage and begins to list all the things which they believe to constitute unreasonable behaviour, the memory suffers from selective amnesia. If all divorce petitions were to be believed, there wouldn't be one happy instance in the entire marriage, and nine times out of ten, people exclude the circumstances that preceded the events in question. David Green commented: "Virtually anyone who has been married for any period of time can produce a list of behaviour which appears sufficiently unreasonable to convince any right-thinking person."

When Rosemary and Stephen agreed to divorce on the ground of her unreasonable behaviour, Stephen's solicitor peered over his glasses, having read the modest catalogue of error and said: "Is that it, then? Can't you think of anything else?" Stephen went home and Rosemary rewrote the list of her *own* unreasonable behaviour to which the solicitor responded: "*That's* better, we can do something with *this*."

Despite appeals to the contrary, the Lord Chancellor refused to introduce the no-fault divorce and so, for the foreseeable future, there must still be evidence of unreasonable behaviour and anyone who makes up the allegations can be prosecuted for perjury. The Solicitors Family Law Association recommends that in petitions based on behaviour, the written allegations should be "kept to the minimum necessary to secure a divorce - which may not be very much, these days".

Much of what passes as unreasonable behaviour would be thrown out of court if the Respondent's version of the same instances were added but, often the first they know of what they stand accused, of is when a copy of the petition arrives on the door mat. At this stage, the outraged Respondent has only one aim and that is to put the record straight by contesting the divorce.

Any decent solicitor should inform the Respondent that what is detailed in the petition will *not* influence the judge over the issues that matter — the eventual settlement and the children - and does not serve their best interests to pursue it. Defended divorces merely drag out the proceedings and increases the costs so it's better the Respondent bites the bullet in order to get it over with as quickly as possible. If someone is determined to see a divorce through, then come hell or high water, nothing is going to stop them. It's just one more of the 99% of divorces to go through undefended.

CHANGES AND QUIRKS IN THE LAW

As we have already discovered, there have been quite a few drastic changes in the laws affecting divorce and many of these might be pertinent to our own case. For this reason, we should never assume that by reading an article or a book that we've got to grips with the finer points of the new legislation. The law in all its glory is long, complex and involves a period of intense study before it can be understood. Even those magazine pieces written by a solicitor can only give a thumb-mail sketch of what these changes may imply for an individual case.

Although you and your partner might have managed to reach an agreement, you would still be best advised to ask a solicitor to draw up and deal with the paperwork, to get the court's seal of approval on what you have decided. To ensure there is no come-back, or one partner reneging on the agreement, the court order needs to be correct and cover all legal contingencies in precise and accurate legal terms — especially any covered by recent amendments. If you don't intend to defend your corner and will allow the divorce to go through without let or hindrance, it may still be in your best interest to consult a solicitor to ensure you're not leaving anything undone, or signing away anything you'll regret at a later date.

For example: a case cited in one of the women's magazines dropped the bombshell that where there had been no concluded financial settlement between a couple divorced four years previously, an ex-wife still had a claim on a legacy her husband received *after* the marriage was dissolved.

This may also apply to any monies won on the lottery or pools if a couple fail to resolve financial matters before the *decree absolute* has granted. Any wealth that has been built up independently since the marriage breakdown may also be taken into consideration, so don't skimp on the legal advice when it comes to financial matters. (In Scotland all capital claims must be made at the time of the divorce and cannot be made afterwards.)

HOW DOES IT AFFECT YOU?
Even if you want to go for an amicable DIY divorce, it is still important to consult a solicitor in the initial stages, and during the stages of submitting the relevant paperwork to the court. Providing his instructions are confined to implementing those issues that have been agreed between you and your partner, costs can be kept to the a minimum. One solicitor cannot, however, act for both parties and a court may be reluctant to recognise any agreed settlement if one of you has not consulted a solicitor at all. In all aspect of divorce the court must be convinced that both parties' interests have been protected. If you have steamed ahead without being fully aware of any changes to the law, this may cause difficulties later ... and you will only have yourself to blame.

VIEWPOINTS FROM THE LAYMAN'S ARMS
The Nicole Kidman – Tom Cruise divorce raised some rather interesting questions about the division of their assets, estimated at £340 million: Kidman's fortune was thought to be half that of her husband's. As an extremely successful, high-earning actress in her own right, should Kidman be entitled to claim against her husband's wealth over and above any settlement made for their adopted children?

Male response
"Nicole Kidman clearly isn't a typical housewife dependent on her partner's earning for her survival. In this case, both partners' assets

should be added up and each given 50% of the total. If the courts award an additional settlement for the adopted children, that should be that. On the surface (and quite unfair, as it happens), the newspapers make this look like plain greed; the extremely wealthy demanding the right to become mega-rich without working for it."

"No way! Tom Cruise was in films making money long before he married her. He has earned his money on his own merit, as has Nicole Kidman. She is not without money and will go on to earn more. What's his is his, and vice versa."

Female response

"Yes, no doubt about it. They had no pre-nuptial agreement — they were marrying for life. Both lots of assets should go into the marital pool and they should both have half — then wrangle about the kids on top of that, i.e. whoever gets care of the kids gets more of the communal pool for doing so."

"No. Because each party has earned via their own individual talents — and at her age she can go on to earn plenty more."

NB: In all fairness, the Cruise-Kidman divorce was ultimately privately handled with the utmost discretion and appears to have no long-lasting and unpleasant repercussions, or unfair financial demands.

Chapter Three

Legal Mud Wrestling

Regardless of your position it is in your best interests to select a family law solicitor whose 'approach is constructive and non-adversarial'. Discard those bias viewpoints of family and friends and make up your mind to accept the responsibility for any decisions you make over your (and, your children's) future. Have a definite picture in your mind about what is important to you and resist the urge to make unrealistic financial demands.

No matter how civilised you and your separating partner set out to be, by the time things have reached the petition stage, hurt and anger will have prompted one (or both) of you to resort to mud-slinging. If either you or your partner are leaving because there's someone else in the frame, you can hardly expect the other to say: "How wonderful, darling, I wish you the best of luck!" Similarly, if the marriage has gone pear-shaped because of a build-up of 'compound issues' the abandoned spouse is not going to hold up their hands and cry "Guilty as charged!"

Regardless of the reason why you're splitting up, neither of you are going to admit it's *your* fault – for the simple reason that you want to believe that it was your partner's behaviour that pushed you into:

- Belting him with the clock
- Having a wild affair with the central heating engineer
- Running into debt
- Turning to drink
- Neglecting the kids
- Giving away his cherished possessions
- Publicly criticising her fashion sense
- Not wanting sex
- Stop trying to communicate
- Turning your back on the whole shooting match

Just as it takes two to tango, it takes two get a divorce. Even if it is extremely difficult for you to understand why your partner suddenly wants to end 10 years of marriage, having a screaming fit or walking out of the door isn't going to bring about any enlightenment.

KEEPING CONTROL

Women find that as soon as they announce that they are considered a divorce, they're met with a wall of silence (disbelief), followed by the television going on (if I ignore it, it won't happen) and a refusal to discuss the problem (bewilderment). Unfortunately, most women confronted with this reaction think to themselves: "Well, if he's *that* bothered, I'll go ahead!" What they don't realise is that the male has gone into that famous cave (*Men Are From Mars, Women Are From Venus*), becoming increasingly distant, unresponsive and pre-occupied. This is not an excuse; it's a well-researched fact.

Women on the receiving end usually scream non-stop abuse or lapse into numbed silence (fear), following by the urge to wreck something (anger) and a prolonged period of silence coupled with a dereliction of housewifely duties (brooding resentment). When a woman is stressed she needs to talk about her feelings and this situation is often the only time in her life she is rendered speechless. He thinks: "If I keep out of the way, it can't degenerate into another shouting match." Result: stalemate.

In situations such as these, *neither* of you is retaining any form of control. This could be the last chance you have to mend the marriage and, even if you've made an irreversible decision to leave, it can still be to your advantage to remain on speaking terms with your ex-.

Josephine was determined not to fall out with her ex- and refused to allow herself to be goaded by any of his temper tantrums, insults or threats. Five years after the divorce they are still on reasonable terms even though Josephine has remarried. "I can't say we're *good* friends but close enough to dog-sit while the other's on holiday, and exchange Christmas and birthday presents. It wasn't the easiest six months I've ever spent but I think it was worth it in the long run even though there weren't any children involved."

WHEN THE GLOVES COME OFF

The legal machinations surrounding divorce are not, however, conducive to civilised and sensible behaviour. Nowhere was this more strongly defined than in the row that enveloped Tom Cruise and Nicole Kidman following the announcement of their separation. Just 48 hours after they had announced an 'amicable separation' and issued a statement stressing 'their great respect for each other', Cruise had filed divorce papers apparently using a legal ploy to avoid paying the maximum in alimony.

According to newspaper reports, Kidman was left humiliated by the action as the couple had only begun talking about a separation a fortnight before the actual split. Although the couple were seen out and about together after their 10th wedding anniversary, Cruise claimed that the 10-year marriage lasted nine years and 11 months, which would effectively save millions of dollars in alimony payments. Californian judges view marriages that go beyond 10 years in a different light: after 10 years, a wife is entitled to be financially supported for life. Should Cruise's petition have been granted, he would have to help his ex- for only half of the duration of the marriage — five years.

As it happened, the couple eventually decided to divorce quickly and sort out the other issues involving the children, money and property at a later date, so commonsense obviously prevailed.

A lawyer is, of course, quite correct in advising his client about any legal loop-holes that can be utilised to safe-guard any assets. Unfortunately, knee-jerk decisions are made at a time when emotions are scrambled and it is very, *very* easy to embark on a course that will cause a great deal of upset and misery. Judging by the relationship *following* their divorce, it is doubtful whether Mick Jagger ever intended to hurt Jerry Hall with his counter-attack claiming that their

Hindu marriage ceremony in Bali wasn't legally valid. Jerry Hall, of course, behaved impeccably but she was obviously devastated to have, what was for her a beautiful and meaningful ceremony, trashed by a lawyer as a gimmicky bit of flim-flam.

Very few of us will ever be involved in multi-million pound divorces but even when the assets are those of Mr and Mrs Average, one party will fight (on the advice of their lawyer) to perverse as much as they can intact. When we stand there bewildered and hurt by the actions of someone we once thought cared for us, we quickly come to realise that, like Nicole Kidman and Jerry Hall found, when the gloves come off, things get very ugly indeed.

You may not feel like being charitable, especially if you're on the receiving end of what you consider to be a 'groundless' divorce, but if your partner's decided to go ahead with the proceedings there's very little you can do about it. Keeping control means that you will respond to any demands or requests in a calm, detached manner.

So:

- Resist the urge to go for everything you can get

- Make concessions over favourite household items

- Don't act out of spite

- Don't object to the request for family pieces to be handed over

- Never make a snap decision — mull it over for a couple of days

- Ignore the opinions/advice of friends and family

Of course, your solicitor will advise you to go for your full entitlement and they wouldn't be doing their job properly if they didn't, but if in your heart of hearts you don't think something is fair, don't agree until you've had time to think it over.

SECONDS OUT ... ROUND ONE

Divorce is all about justification — by both parties. A man can always justify his reasons behind having a fling with Ms X from Personnel — as can his wife if she's been caught in *flagrante delicto* with a neighbour's husband after he'd been round to mend the shed. The difference is that men will maintain that the 'fling' didn't involve any emotional involvement (which makes it okay); for women it was a meaningful relationship (which makes it okay).

If we discount domestic violence and/or a wide permutation of sexually-related reasons, most divorce petitions (if they were totally honest) would look pretty flimsy. Being fed-up to the back teeth with unsavoury personal habits, or a continuous public undermining of confidence may not, in themselves, be grounds for divorce but they may be a mere tip of the matrimonial iceberg against which your partner is about to sail his/her unsuspecting liner. If the collision is violent enough, the ship may go down with all hands on board, without a lifeboat in sight.

Make a complete list of all the reasons why you believe you cannot reasonably be expected to live with your husband/wife. Now record all the irritating habits s/he has — and on the opposite side make a corresponding list of your own. Lawyer, Vanessa Lloyd Platt commented in her book, *Secrets of Relationship Success*, many women claim that they do not have irritating habits, while their partners have so many. Men, on the other hand, are generally more easy going and don't notice the things that would drive a woman round the bend. So sit down and draw up your list but remember:

- Keep it simple

- Keep it short

- Keep it clean

- Keep it fair

- And no hitting below the belt

Round One ... is the issuing of the divorce petition and, if you're on the receiving end, you might just be left wondering to whom the hell this bit of legal jargon refers! It isn't necessary to make your partner out to be the villain of the piece; it's quite sufficient to show clearly and concisely why you wish to end the marriage.

ALL'S FAIR IN DIVORCE AND WAR

If a court has to consider any question involving the residence or upbringing of a child, the law states that the child's welfare must be the first and paramount consideration. "A court is not entitled to consider whether, from any other point of view, the claims of the father may be superior to those of the mother, or the claims of the mother superior to the father" (*Splitting Up* — David Green).

As a result, one parent is going to be left feeling that he or she has 'lost' both financially and as far as access to the children are concerned. Inevitably, children will suffer more when hostilities are fuelled by continual court-room bickering so your prime concern should be keeping this to a minimum.

Nevertheless, one barrister who asked not be named in a *Daily Telegraph* report claimed that judges *were still* biased against husbands and that in a typical divorce, the court would decide that the children should live with their mother. This means that once a wife grew tired/bored/disillusioned with her husband, she could force him out of his own home, since by rule of thumb whoever gets the children gets the house.

Subsequently, when the father tries to see his children, the ex-wife's new chap refuses him access to a property to which he may still be contributing to the mortgage. As an absent parent (i.e. the one legally booted out) he must continue to pay maintenance for the children and may also have to pay maintenance to his ex- even though she is cohabiting with a new man-friend. As legal editor, Joshua Rozenberg observed, however, statistically, children are more likely to be abused by their stepfather than by a natural parent and currently there are moves afoot to uphold the law in favour of fathers who are being refused access to their children.

The Solicitors Family Law Association has been looking at ways of 'helping people through divorce in ways that minimise the distress and acrimony' but this is scant compensation to the husband or wife who has been forced out of their own home through a divorce that was not of their own making. This illustrates why it is essential for you to keep control of the proceedings since you and your partner are the only ones who can ensure there a civilised outcome to the whole unfortunate business. It would have been an interesting exercise to see whether there would still be the level of antipathy between divorcing couples if the Government *had* introduced the 'no fault' divorce.

PRE-NUPTIAL AGREEMENTS

The subject of pre-nuptial agreements has been around for a while but it hit the headlines prior to the Catherine Zeta Jones-Michael Douglas wedding when the couple had difficulties in reaching some kind of settlement over who got what should the marriage fail, although the gossip-mongers failed to mention that this document was later torn up. Many might have felt that this was hardly the most romantic of issues on the eve of a wedding but others will have had more than a passing interest in the outcome.

The head of family law at Mishcon de Reya believes there is a strong case for making the 'pre-nup' - the essential ingredient of any Hollywood break-up — legally binding in Britain. "Pre-nups are not just for the rich and famous. They can help people appreciate what their prospective spouse's attitude to money is. You would not enter into a commercial transaction without a contract. Marriage is a business contract with emotion laid on top."

In reality, it is not unreasonable for someone to wish to protect their own personal assets that were accrued *before* the relationship began, especially in the case of a highly successful and lucrative career or family business. Those contemplating a second marriage are more likely to consult their lawyer over the possibility of making a pre-nuptial agreement in order to protect themselves from being taken to the cleaners for a second time.

There is, of course, a major problem: in England and Wales

the law pays little heed to them. In other countries they are commonplace and legally recognised providing they have been prepared correctly and in full knowledge of the financial circumstances of both parties. However, in Britain the courts still regard them as contrary to public policy, despite the fact that the Solicitors Family Law Association, which represents 5,000 specialist lawyers, says that couples *should* be able to decide in advance how their assets would be divided on divorce instead of waiting until the courts do so for them.

The family lawyers argue that greater clarity and certainty resulting from such agreements might encourage more couples to marry in the first place. A spokesman said: "Making a pre-marital agreement may not seem to be a very romantic thing to do in the run-up to a wedding, but for some couples it can amount to sensible financial planning.

David Salter, the chairman of the Solicitors Family Law Association's law reform committee, said there was a growing sense of unease among divorcing couples about the unpredictability of the courts' approach to the financial aspects of divorce. "There is a need, at times, to protect the weaker person in a marriage, but when a couple make an arrangement in the full knowledge of its effect, they should be entitled to have it upheld by the courts."

There is a subtle indication, however, that attitudes might be changing, since in 2002, a pre-marital agreement was largely upheld by a deputy High Court judge on the basis that the couple had freely agreed to the deal and 'there had been no unforeseen change in circumstances leading to any injustice'.

Faced with the cold hard facts that one in three marriages finish in the divorce court, it is becoming increasingly obvious that financial agreements of this nature may actively encourage those couples living together to make that extra commitment. Few people in their right mind, however, are going to risk losing everything again simply because the law can't get its act together to uphold a properly drawn up pre-nuptial agreement.

Cohabiting is a growing trend among those in the 30+ age groups, largely because these are the people who are more likely to have established a sound financial lifestyle prior to a second marriage. It is one of the advantages that cohabitees can enjoy: the security of a legally effective financial agreement, when married couples have no means of safe-guarding their own personal assets.

With hindsight, would you have:

- considered a pre-nuptial agreement to safeguard your own assets?

- had any problem signing a pre-nuptial agreement at your prospective partner's suggestion?

- felt that it undermined your relationship?

FINANCIAL SETTLEMENTS

On the other side of the legal coin, following a judgement in the House of Lords in October 2000, women now stand to gain a greater share of their husband's assets should the marriage fail. Wives who have not worked during the marriage but who have brought up the children and looked after the family home, are now expected to receive a more substantial settlement.

Formerly, these were restricted to a house and a maintenance fund that placed a limit on financial settlements. It often meant that ex-wives only received a fraction of what the couple's assets were worth when they were together. The biggest shake-up in the divorce laws for 30 years means that judges must make settlements on a far more equal basis. And for the first time, it recognises that a mother makes as big a contribution to the marriage as a husband who goes out to work and earns the money.

The ruling followed a four-year court battle between a farmer and his former wife over a farm business they built up over 33 years. The case ended with the couple facing a combine legal bill of £850,000. At first the former wife was awarded a lump sum of £800,000 as a one-off payment, but she took the case to the Appeal Court, which increased her award by £700,000. The husband appealed against the decision and the case went to the House of Lords.

When one 'footballer's wife' appealed against a maintenance payment of £212,500 awarded by the High Court, her solicitors justified her action by explaining that although the settlement was more than her reasonable needs, it did not allow her to put enough money aside to buy security for the future, especially in view of her husband's long-term career prospects. In this case, the appeal judges took the novel step of ruling that income can be used to build up capital and ruled that the footballer was to pay his ex-wife and children a total of £444,000 per year for the next four years. The ex-wife would be expected to invest all but £150,000 in a nest egg for the future, as her former husband's earning capacity may be considerably lower four years hence.

Formally, when assessing financial settlements, judges would have considered the perimeters set out in the 1973 Matrimonial Causes Act which included age; income earning capacity; length of the marriage; marital standard of living; and financial needs and obligations. It was then up to the presiding judge as to how to exercise that discretion in the division of assets. As one solicitor pointed out, however, "The presumption now will be that assets will automatically be split 50/50, and cases will now have to debate why the assets *shouldn't* be divided in this way."

Do you think that:
- non-working wives should be treated as equal partners?
- house-husbands should be treated as equal partners?
- husbands should be expected to pay a 50/50 settlement if his wife walks out?
- the stay-at-home partner makes as big a contribution to the relationship?

The focus of most cases is to satisfy the reasonable needs of a partner (usually, but not necessarily, the wife) consistent with the couple's lifestyle and the partner's ability to pay. A spouse has an automatic right to claim maintenance (which can be for an indefinite duration), capital and a share in property. It should not, however, be taken for granted that in every case the 'starting point' for the division of assets of the couple should be equality. It would also be wrong to assume that money spent on a hobby (particularly collecting — antiques, stamps, vintage wine) will not be classed as assets should they have a recognised accumulative value.

PENSIONS

In the past, pension funds have often been the largest and most contentious asset in a divorce case but couples who lodged divorce proceedings after 1st December 2000 were eligible for pension sharing. This new ruling entitles one partner to claim a share of their spouse's pension as part of the divorce settlement by taking part of the value of a spouse's pension as a 'debit' and give it to he other as a 'credit'. One law firm who specialised in Family Law admitted that there were a large number of prospective divorcees who held back until after the deadline before beginning proceedings in order to benefit from the new laws.

What we must not lose sight of with these new changes, is that we are not *automatically* entitled to a half share of a husband or wife's pension upon divorce. In sharing out the matrimonial assets, the court will take into account all the various factors such as the length of the marriage, the age of the couple as well as the needs and resources available. The pension fund (of either spouse) may be one of the biggest assets where a couple have been married for a long time and are reaching retirement age. For a much younger couple in their 20s or 30s with only a few years marriage under their belt, the court is unlikely to take much notice of pension funds that will not be payable for many years.

In any divorce proceedings, both husband and wife are required to disclose all their assets. In the case of a long-term marriage where the wife has a more substantial pension fund, a husband may find that the new laws work to his advantage and that *he* is entitled to a sharing order against his *wife's* pension. Pension sharing means that the court can order a percentage of a pension fund to be transferred to the other party to be held in their own right.

This will mean, for example, that a wife would now have a pension of her own, either with her ex-husband's pension company, or transferred to another pension company of her own choice. Once this agreement has been incorporated into a Court Order, if the husband were to die before drawing his pension, the ex-wife would still be entitled to receive the benefits under her own separate pension fund even if she remarries.

Understanding pension details

Because of their complexity, pensions are 'notoriously difficult' to assess and for this reason we would be well advised to have a solicitor deal with the companies involved. There are many different types of pension, depending on whether it is a private one, a final salary pension, funded or non-funded — and each one will have a different set of rules and procedures. Your solicitor will write to the companies to obtain full details of the pensions involved and, unless the amounts are negligible, you really need to fully understand what is involved before agreeing to any settlement.

Although there will be a certain amount of security for those getting a divorce after many years of marriage, knowing they will not have to start from scratch saving for their retirement, one financial advisor warned of the practical problems in *rebuilding* the pension. Once a pension has been divided, divorcees will find there are limited options open to them, particularly is they are nearing retirement age. Under present rulings, the 15% of annual earning limit on contributions into an occupational scheme will make rebuilding a fund extremely difficult for older savers. It is therefore very important to discuss any settlement with an independent advisor.

Transferring assets

Another area that will require professional advice is the allocation of the couple's share portfolio. A husband and wife can generally transfer assets between themselves without any tax liability since for capital gains tax purposes, assets are treated as being transferred between spouses on a 'gain-no loss' basis. This treatment continues during the rest of the tax year of separation even if the couple are no longer living together, or until the *decree absolute* is granted —

if this is before the end of the tax year. There are special rules in respect of assets transferred as part of a divorce settlement, and where any substantial assets are changing hands it is advisable to discuss this with a financial advisor as any tax liability will depend on the timing of the asset transfer.

COHABITING

There are numerous myths surrounding that misnomer 'common-law' partner; the greatest one being that once a couple have lived together for a while, they automatically become entitled to the same legal rights as a couple who are legally married. According to the Institute for Social & Economic Research, cohabitation accounts for 70% of first partnerships but within two years of cohabiting, nearly 90% end up marrying their partner. The research concludes, however, that cohabiting couples are far less likely to stay together than married couples – only a third of unmarried parents' relationships survive until their children are 16 years old, compared with more than two thirds of married couples.

Since these relationships have fewer safeguards, cohabitees have the advantage under the present law to make cohabitation agreements, and it is obviously in their best interest to do so, especially if there are children involved. Like pre-nuptial agreements, cohabitation agreements hardly rank very high in the romantic stakes but whereas when a marriage breaks up the less well off party (usually but not necessarily the woman) can claim a lump-sum settlement or a share of the property, cohabitees do not have this right. Anyone, male or female, contemplating a live-in relationship without marriage should seriously consider their position before downgrading their earning capacity, even if they are joint owners of the property in which they live.

Understanding the legal position

Imogen Clout, a family lawyer and the author of *The Which? Guide to Living Together*, urges all unmarried couples to sign a

'Living Together Agreement' that sets out what would happen if the relationship should end. It sets out 'transitional arrangements' that couples living together should put in place, such as selling the home immediately, paying outstanding bills and dividing the balance of a joint account.

The Living Together campaign by Advicenow.org.uk, a legal advice service, is being funded by the Department for Constitutional Affairs, to help cohabiting couples understand the pitfalls of a live-in relationship without marriage. Increasing numbers of men and women are choosing *not* to get married and according to Vanessa Lloyd Platt, "Men who are already wedding phobic are terrified about draconian divorce laws will now simply refuse to marry."

According to Martin Jones, the director of Advicenow.org.uk, new research shows that despite all the publicity to the contrary, six in 10 people still believe that couples who have lived together for a while have the same rights as married couples. And more than six in 10 women think that they have a legal right to financial support from their partner if they have been living together more than five years. Seven in 10 people believe that the father of a child automatically has a right to make decisions about his child's future, regardless of whether he is married or not. Not of these is true.

From a woman's perspective, she can live with a man for 25 years, change her name by deed poll, bear three children and give up her job to look after him but if there is no legal marriage, there can be no legal claim against him — or his estate if he dies without formally making a will in her favour. The same goes for a man. If he does not marry, he will have no financial claim if the relationship breaks down. This fact should also be borne in mind by those growing numbers who were 'handfasted' under the mistaken belief that a New Age or pagan wedding is legally binding.

If the relationship is only of a short duration, then one partner can find themselves out on the street and paying half of the legal costs if the judge decides that one partner's right to the capital is greater that the other's right to remain in the house. Should you find yourself in the position of splitting up from a live-in lover, it will be necessary for you to prepare details of:

1. Property of any sort which they have acquired together
2. Property which is jointly owned by them
3. The contributions they have made to the property held by, or in the name of their fellow cohabitee.
4. The values of any property and of any outstanding mortgages or debts on it, and of any taxes or costs which may arise if it is sold.

Both parties should keep documented evidence of all financial contributions to the household, with recipes where necessary, so they can be taken into account when it comes to dividing up the money. That means paying — with verifiable statements — the mortgage, rather than paying the weekly shopping bill. An application can be made to the court for an injunction to prevent the premature disposal of the property and, as with any other couple, the cohabitee should also consider changing their wills and serving notices ending any joint tenancy of the property.

CHANGES IN THE LAW

A 2001 Government Green Paper, *Supporting Families,* contained proposals that pre-nuptial agreements and contracts be given legal status. The proposal is that they should be binding on those who wish to have them. The proposals include a safeguard that contracts would not be enforceable unless both parties had taken independent advice and fully disclosed their financial position beforehand and be signed at least 21 days before the marriage takes place. By 2004, a £100,000 Government-funded campaign was launched to combat the legal pitfalls surrounding cohabitation, which sets out the steps the couple can take to safe-guard their own personal assets.

Although the Government has, so far, refused to implement Part II of the Family Law Act that would have allowed couples to obtain a 'no fault divorce', lawyers will continue to put pressure on the Government regarding the need for drastic improvements in matrimonial law, so the 'no fault divorce' may be back on the agenda before too long.   In the meantime, until the Government decides to implement new legislation, we are stuck with the existing laws.

HOW DOES THIS AFFECT YOU?

❖ According to the latest media gossip, rich husbands looking to divorce their wives are being warned by legal and financial experts to leave England and Wales, which could soon become the most expensive place in the world to sever marital ties. One of the main factors leading to costly divorces is that, while in countries such as German and France, property owned before marriage is normally excluded from settlements, in England and Wales it is all part of the pot shared out between husband and wife.

❖ For cohabiting gay couples, however, legislation is being put in place to recognise the fact that they cannot marry. The arrangements, which are scheduled to become law in 2005, will mean that gay couples can register their partnership in a civil ceremony so they can enjoy the same legal rights as married couples. The new rights contained in the Civil Partnerships Bill, will not be extended to cohabiting, heterosexual couples because they are able to marry should they choose. Although the legislation covers only England and Wales, it is due to be extended to Scotland and Northern Ireland.

❖ Maintenance payments are a frequent bone of contention between former partners, even if payments are missed for reasons beyond the contributor's control. Some financial advisors are urging divorced and separated couples to consider insuring their former partner's ability to pay maintenance. Many parents who are divorcing will painstakingly negotiate housing arrangements, maintenance payments and pensions but overlook financial protection for their children in the event of their former partner's death, critical illness, accident, sickness or unemployment. There are many schemes that will provide this type of cover and a small monthly payment negotiated at the time of divorce can make all the difference in the world to both parties' peace of mind.

❖ Family law is under review all the time and never assume you are in full grasp of the facts on the strength of an article read in a magazine or newspaper.

VIEWPOINTS FROM THE LAYMAN'S ARMS

When a wealthy couple were divorced she was awarded more than £3 million in settlements that included the couple's renovated period country house set in 15 acres and a holiday flat in Ocean Boulevard, Florida. She claimed that the £3.1 million settlement would yield only £100,00 a year, which was far too low given the lifestyle she was entitled to expect. She applied to the High Court for another £1 million in recognition of her work in bringing up their children who have since grown up and left home. Should the ex-wife be treated as an equal partner?

Male opinion:

"Yes, of course she should, but that isn't the issue here. The issue is should she be given an extra £1 million on top of the £3.1 million awarded by the court? Whatever the £3.1 million may or may not yield per year is neither here nor there, she was awarded this sum by the court and that ought to be that. She should not be entitled to expect a certain minimum lifestyle in the future either. What happens in the future is not important—only here and now.

"Had the children still been in her care this would have put a different slant on events, but they have grown up and left home. The same goes for her claim for extra money in recognition for her work in bringing up the children in the past. That was in the past and presumably was taken into account when she was awarded the £3.1 million. And how much of this settlement would effect he children's inheritance?"

"Should the High Court have the power to increase settlements? I would hope that they would also have the power to *decrease* them too, as they see fit. It sounds very much to me that she already has more than an equal share of her ex-husband's assets, and now she would like the clothes he stands up in as well. This should have been split more equally, as happens in most divorce cases, but I get the impression she is claiming for greed not need."

Female opinion:
"Actually, I think she should but I find this case more difficult because, to be honest, I *do* think she is being greedy. That said, if I were in her position I too would go for every penny I could get my hands on. After 35 years of marriage, you would expect that you were going to live with that partner for the rest of your life, and therefore share equally in the lifestyle his earnings would generate. For that disappointment alone I would want to claw back as much of his money as I could — then I'd take up with a 'toy-boy', go to live somewhere in the sun, and live a life of luxury and excess!"

"If the husband has an estimated £12 million, then the wife should get rather more than £3 million. If 'average' couples are allocated a 50/50 split, this should apply to everyone, regardless of status or income."

Chapter Four

Telling the family

If you thought discussing divorce with your partner was difficult enough, wait until the news becomes public. You may think that it's no business of anyone's but your own but it's not just the husband and wife who are involved in divorce proceedings. It also concerns quite a lot of other people - including children, both sets of grandparents, the rest of the family and friends — all of whom will feel duty bound to put in their four penny worth of advice.

So be warned — things *can* get worse.

TELLING THE CHILDREN

In the UK alone over 160,000 children under the age of 16 are involved with the separation and divorce of their parents. Those who cope best with the break-up of the family are the ones who are able to see the 'absent' parent as often as possible, free from the anxiety of a guilt trip from the parent with whom they live. If the new domestic arrangements can be as flexible as possible, then so much the better for everyone concerned.

No matter how flexible your arrangements with your children and your ex-, these should be observed at all cost. Resist the urge to offer something better when its your ex's turn to take them out; we all know that children can be mercenary and will opt for the more appealing 'treat'. If you mastermind this, don't be surprised if the situation disintegrates into a slanging match on the doorstep if the kids aren't there when your ex- turns up.

Conversely, if you've made a promise to take your children out make sure you turn up, otherwise the hurt and humiliation suffered under the gloating eye of your ex- will be unbearable and gives her/him the ammunition for point scoring. Up until now, there has been little the courts could do to enforce visiting arrangements against a parent who is determined to obstruct them and in all honesty such parental situations were much more common than the agony aunts would have us believe. The much-publicised plight of fathers denied access to their children has been brought to public attention by the antics of an organisation called 'Fathers 4 Justice' and the blistering attack by one of the UK's most senior family judges. Mr Justice Munby's comments came at a time of growing protests against the decisions of the family courts in favour of the mother, with well-known fathers, including Sir Bob Geldof and the Prince of Wales, also criticising the system for being weighed against fathers.

Following the disruption during Prime Minister's Question Time by Fathers 4 Justice throwing purple flour into the Commons, the chairman of the Family Law Bar Association said that the courts should take children away from mothers who flout contact orders by refusing to let them see their father. Philip Moor, QC suggested that a few high-profile rulings in appropriate cases would send a message to other mothers.

Family lawyers are becoming increasingly more 'fed up' with Government inaction in this area. They believe that incidents such as Batman and Robin staging a rooftop protest at the High Court, or Spider-Man's six days on a 100ft crane near Tower Bridge (which won him a runners-up place in a Channel 4 viewer's poll for the most significant political figure of the year) were giving family law a 'pretty bad press'. As a result of all this pressure, we may see some drastic changes in the law in the not too distant future.

The women's magazines have all sorts of counsellors giving advice on how to tell children that a divorce is imminent but in the real world it doesn't happen like that. Most parents don't get the opportunity to sit down quietly to talk about what's going on, let alone arranging for both of them to be there when the bomb's dropped. Even young children are more than likely to be aware of what's going on long before either of their parents get around to explaining things and in the majority of cases, the domestic strife leading up to the bust-up is probably more traumatic than the actual splitting up of the family.

As Sheila remembers: "Children are much more perceptive and resilient than we give them credit for. The important thing is not to treat them any differently than you've always done. If you're a family who thrive on hugs and physical contact, fine, but with a normally undemonstrative family having a parent all over you like a rash can be extremely confusing. I just left and told my boys we would be moving house and that their father wasn't coming with us. Now in their thirties, both are happily married and successful in business."

Jayne made a hurried exit from a violent marriage with the words. "*Get into the car because we were going to Grandma's.* When he asked why the car was piled high with our belongings, I told him that Daddy was an evil bastard and that he'd hit Mummy for the last time. Within just a few days on my mother's farm he was a happy relaxed child, who was sleeping properly for the first time in years and at 20 is now training for a management position in the catering industry."

Richard tried to retain the banter there'd always been between father and son. "The atmosphere at home was such that I just said 'Sorry about the upset, old chap. We'll get it all sorted out, don't you worry. Now I'm just off to murder your Mother'. I've had as little as possible to do with my ex-wife but I've maintained a good relationship with my son even though it wasn't always made easy for me. He's now finished at University and we go sailing whenever we can."

In many instances, parents will wait until the children are old enough to leave home before petitioning for divorce. Figures from the Office for National Statistics indicate that the trend is rising for divorce among couples who have been married for 30 years or more.

"When the kids have gone and you look at the person with whom you're supposed to be spending the next 30 years, something clicks in and you think 'Not bloody likely!'" said Margot a young-looking 55 year old. "It was difficult to explain to my son and daughter that I needed my own life because all they kept on asking was 'Why don't you love Dad anymore? What's he done?' It was hard to give my reasons without putting any guilt on them; that we'd stopped loving each other years ago and I was only waiting for them to leave home so that I could."

Just because children have reached an age of relative maturity, it doesn't mean that they are going to understand why their parents wish to get a divorce. Most of their classmates or colleagues will probably come from a broken marriage but it's different when the divorcing parents are your own. There's a whole new set of values to be examined, particularly if one parent has been having an affair with someone else. We all know how impossible it is to visualise our own parents having sex and so the young can be forgiven for thinking that a middle-aged parent's sex drive is gross!

Research recently published by the Centre for Research on the Family, Kinship and Childhood, however, reveals that in comparison with previous research 15 years earlier "when there were sad tales of children desperately wanting their parents to get back together, young people no longer felt that their lives were ruined by their parents' divorce.".

WHO GETS THE CHILDEN?

Be careful about making promises you may not be able to keep. All arrangements and orders for children are essentially concerned with their interest — not yours. Under normal circumstances most children land up in the primary care of their mothers; fathers awarded care are still the exception. In exceptional cases, however, courts have given primary care to a father where the mother was judged to be mentally unstable, judged to be an unfit mother due to an advanced stage of drug abuse, or obsessed with a particular religious sect. They have also given it where a 12-year old daughter flatly refused to live with her mother. Things *are* slowly beginning to change and the new 'child rights' laws will be seen as a concession to fathers' groups such as Fathers 4 Justice and Families Need Fathers. But in the meantime, refrain from making any promises to your children that may have to be broken through no fault of your own.

Whatever your own attitude to your partner, it is essential that children are not given the feeling that the break-up has in any way been caused by them. Both parents need to bottle their personal antipathy and provide practical information about any changes to the family's domestic arrangements, i.e. where they will be living, what arrangements are being made for them to spend time with their mother/father, and assured there will be room for Teddy and Badger at the new house.

Needless to say, the parent awarded the residence order will be the one who fields most of the questions. The younger the child, the simpler the answers need to be. Older children may give the impression of being 'cool' about the whole thing but don't overlook the fact that they are probably putting a mask on the hurt. The most trivial and stupid of things will spark off tears and tantrums (and that's only the parents!), so prepare for a bumpy ride.

Maintaining a good relationship

Realistically, we've got enough on our own plate at this stage of a divorce and a whinging kid wanting to know why its blue socks haven't been washed, can be the incident that has you reaching for the Prozac.

Obviously, much depends on the reasons behind a divorce but putting aside violence and drug abuse, a good relationship with your ex- can pay dividends. Of course, if you're determined that you're going to be as obstructive as possible when it comes to his/ her contact with the children, then this obviously says much more about *you* than it does about them.

Divorced couples who maintain an adult attitude towards each other can often make tolerable 'friends' especially if they're willing to act as babysitter while you take a well-deserved weekend at the health club, or s/he's suddenly called away on business.

Consider the pluses:
- You have an unpaid babysitter and/or house minder

- You know with whom your children are staying
-
- You don't have to feel you're abdicating responsibility
-
- You don't have to feel guilty about leaving them behind

Parenting doesn't cease to be a joint responsibility because the parents have divorced — and hey, no one said it was going to be easy. Agreed the first few months *will* be prickly and there will be lots of raw emotional patches for all of you, but if you can try to re-member that each of your children will react differently to their new situation and to keep the lines of communication open.

THE ABSENT PARENT
Make no bones about it, children are expert manipulators and the absent parent often finds itself in a position of having to compete in the popularity stakes with their former husband or wife. Of course, it is difficult to understand why your children are taking sides by playing one parent off against the other but this is *the norm not the exception.* Be prepared for it and no matter how hurtful it seems, don't rise to the bait.

Old children appear to align with the same-sex parent and often express anger towards the other parent whom they blame for the divorce — and anything else that comes to mind at the time! Don't be too ready to blame your ex- for influencing them either, children can manage this quite efficiently on their own.

After a divorce it often happens that children go 'wild' and unmanageable. These problems arise in feelings of poor self-esteem, suppressed anger and/or resentment, a sense of loss or rejection. It also happens that this is the only time a warring couple get to talk to each other when the absent father gets a frantic phone call to "come round and sort this kid out before I kill him". Unfairly the absent father is required to appear and lay down the law over something he's been excluded from until the situation has reached crisis point. Often the first he gets to hear about the problem is when he arrives at the police station or hospital.

This type of situation went one step further in undermining the basic rights of the absent parent when judges in the Appeal Court ruled that a former wife could start a new life in New Zealand with the couple's four-year-old daughter. The ex-husband had spent £40,000 in his battle to keep his daughter in Britain and the president of the Equal Parenting Council observed: "This means it will be business as usual: mothers will still be able to take children out of the jurisdiction against their father's wishes. This case was unique in that [the ex-husband] had had frequent contact with his daughter and shared almost 50% of parenting time."

After the marriage collapsed in 1997, his former wife took the child to New Zealand but was ordered to return her to Britain by a court in Auckland. In 2000, however, a Cambridge County Court permitted her to take the child abroad again, and it was against this ruling that the father had appealed. "She's living on the other side of the world; I've spoken to her on the telephone for just four minutes. I have no address, no phone number, I don't know where she is."

Matt O'Connor, founder of Fathers 4 Justice, is highly critical of the system: "You have to prove who's the better parent, and who's the worst, and it becomes a mud-slinging match ... at one point I was seeing my kids 11 hours a month at a contact centre." A year later, he and his former wife reached agreement outside the courts. "It was no thanks to the grotesque legal system and I feel very angry still. I spent £10,000 going through the courts, but I get on fine with my ex-wife and I have two beautiful children."

It was ironic, he said in an interview with the *Daily Telegraph*, that now he had all the access he wanted to his sons, his time was constrained by battling on behalf of other fathers. As a result, under the new proposals drawn up by senior judges, the divorcing couple will be required to agree a 'parenting plan', which spells out the necessity for children to spend plenty of time with their fathers as well as their mothers. Mothers who refuse to comply could find fathers' access to their children increased.

Judges say the proposals will reduce the number of child contact cases in the family courts by up to 75%.

TELLING YOUR PARENTS

If you thought explaining things to your children was tough, then trying to put your point of view across to your parents, or parent-in-law in a sensible and erudite manner. It's quite surprising just how vehement their reaction can be, even towards their *own children* when you raise the subject of divorce.

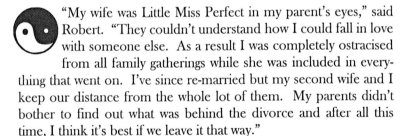 "My wife was Little Miss Perfect in my parent's eyes," said Robert. "They couldn't understand how I could fall in love with someone else. As a result I was completely ostracised from all family gatherings while she was included in every- thing that went on. I've since re-married but my second wife and I keep our distance from the whole lot of them. My parents didn't bother to find out what was behind the divorce and after all this time, I think it's best if we leave it that way."

Robert's second wife is now pregnant with his parent's first grandchild but he still doesn't see any reasons to change his mind about re-establishing contact, so they are completely unaware of the imminent arrival of the baby. As far as he's concerned, they made their choice in supporting his ex-wife, and his case is by no means unusual. Parental attitudes are one of those stretches of uncharted water that often throw up some surprising and devastating re- actions — just when you least need any further complications.

On the other side of the coin, grandparents often find them- selves in the position of being denied contact with grandchildren who are in the primary care of a daughter-in-law and experience the same difficulties as the absent parent. They may apply to the court for contact but this will only be granted where the court is satisfied that contact is in the interest of the children. For example, where:

1] the parent who was a child of the grandparents has died, disappeared, or for some reason is not available to exercise his or her own rights, or
2] there is a positive relationship already established between grandparents and child.

"Grandparents who are not able to see their grandchildren because their *own* child will not allow it should not imagine that the law necessarily gives them a back-door right to change a situation which flows from the fragility of their own family relationships," writes solicitor David Green.

The court may take the view that it is not in the children's best interest to go against the wishes of the parent. However, a senior civil servant and his wife are preparing to fight their daughter in court for the right to 'communicate' with their 2-year old grandson via Christmas and birthday presents. According to the Family Law Association, a growing number of grandparents are applying for contact orders so there may be more changes in the law before too long.

A FAMILY AFFAIR
Short of sending round a newsletter to the rest of the family, think long and hard about what, when and if you want them to know, because even the closest of families can throw up some surprising reactions. If you come from a close-knit family, these unsuspected feelings could undermine your resolve to go through with the divorce, or frighten you into abandoning the idea. One of the biggest mistakes we make is assuming that those closest to us understand and accept the reasons behind our dissatisfaction or unrest. Often we take the attitude that if they really cared about us, they wouldn't interfere in what we want to do with our lives.

"My sister wouldn't leave me in the same room with her husband," recalls Carole. "She really thought that I'd pounce on him as soon as I got the opportunity. We finished up having a right royal row over it - which wasn't helped by my comment that he wouldn't be an option if he were the last bloke on the planet. I was passed caring by that time but she still hasn't forgiven me."

Barbara's family refused to have her husband in the house. "Even though it was a perfectly civilised break up — we just wanted to go our separate ways — they were awful to Brian. They wouldn't believe he hadn't done anything wrong. If I'd been able to announce publicly that he was a wife batterer or child abuser, they'd have beer as happy as Larry!"

Elderly grandparents, especially those from within a strong religious community, can also be difficult. Whilst this should not be a deciding factor, there needs to be some consideration over the right way of dealing with the problem or whether it should be left to someone else to break the news. Within orthodox religion the issue may be non-negotiable and so you may find it necessary to go ahead without the support of your family or religious community.

"My grandmother kept on screeching that we'd never had a divorce in the family," said Jonathon remembering his matriarchal upbringing. "We'd had serial adulterers, illegitimate babies and domestic violence but never a divorce. The old lady was beside herself with temper and threatened to cut me out of her will. As there were three children and nine grandchildren, I figured it wouldn't matter too much and told to go ahead. The next thing I knew she'd had a heart attack and the family blamed me for that, too."

Take a moment to reflect on the long-term repercussions of your actions.

- Would your divorce cause a major family row or upset?

- Is there a particular member of the family (of whom you are particularly fond) who would be deeply upset or offended by your divorce?

- Do you have the personal courage and strength to cope with a family rift?

- Is there a family friend or member who can intercede on your behalf?

- Would a divorce lead to exclusion from your family/ community?

At this point it isn't necessary to have all the answers to these questions but it's a good time to reflect on the changes we could bring about in the lives of others. Bear in mind that even those who come to terms with the changes and actively support any decision we make, can still feel confused by the reasons for the divorce because, all of a sudden, we are not the person they thought they knew. Our families, more often than not, want the best for us, but at the same time *they* will be fearful of losing something of the past in the divorce process.

Understanding these viewpoints is just another aspect of keeping control over our personal feelings and not be steam-rollered into doing something we'll regret because of guilt.

THE FRIENDSHIP FACTOR
Often it's our best friends who know what's going on long before anyone else. Close personal friends are the ones to whom we confide our secrets or misgivings. They are the people who act as our sounding-boards and help us through the agonising over whether divorce is an option, or just a drama-queen reaction to the fact that our partner forgot an important event. These are the few to whom we can pour out our innermost secrets because we trust them not to blab, no matter how juicy the gossip.

The term 'friend' is often casually applied to anyone with whom we interact at work, college, the gym, or club when, in fact, they should be more aptly labelled 'acquaintances'. Even some friendships, however, set their own perimeters. We all have people whose company we enjoy because their sparkle adds to the quality of our own lives but they are not the sort of people in whom we confide. We know we can never trust them with our secrets because we are aware of how indiscreet they can be about others in our circle.

Evaluating friendship

- They continually approve of your actions
- They're always good fun
- They make no demands on you
- They never criticise
- They reflect your own perceived social standing
- They tell you the truth even if it may hurt
- It's a relationship based on honesty and trust
- They will always be there is times of trouble
- They don't always agree with you, for the right reasons.

If you place the emphasis of friendship on the first five points, you may find a considerable amount of disillusionment around the corner because these people can rarely resist gossip. By keeping your own counsel you can keep a measure of control over what other people know about your affairs. You wouldn't be the first to find out that your partner intended to divorce you via a 'disinterested' third party who thought you ought to know.

There will be other surprises: "I've lost count of the number of women who, on announcing their intention to divorce, finding out from their closest friend that the husband had tried his hand in the early days of marriage, or when the wife was expecting the first baby. New husbands appear to think that the best friend is fair game and comes with the territory," was one marriage counsellor's observation.

ON A NEED TO KNOW BASIS

Although there is no need to trumpet your divorce from the roof-tops, it may be provident to inform those who come into contact with your children on a regular basis. A confidential word in the ear of the head teacher at school and any social or youth organis-ers could explain any uncharacteristic behaviour that may occur. You only need to divulge as much as you want anyone to know but it would help if the school understands that it may be your ex-who collects the children on alternate weekends.

It also helps if you can have a quiet word with your employer so that they understand the reason behind the requests for time off work. Most will be sympathetic and can judge for themselves who among your colleagues needs to know until you're ready to go public.

Moving from 'maybe" to 'definite'.

The 'need to know basis' also governs when the divorce moves from 'maybe' to 'definite'. Gerald knew that his wife had finally accepted his request for a divorce when she agreed to tell his step-daughter they were splitting up. Rosemary breathed a sigh of relief when Stephen finally told his mother they were divorcing. There appears to be an indefinable line in the sand which, once crossed, means that the intention to divorce comes out into the open. Until this line has been crossed, however, one partner may refuse to be-lieve that the other is serious.

This is usually a time of great tension for both parties when normal, everyday annoyances are blown up out of all proportion to erupt into full scale rows. It is also the times when you will both say things that should be left unsaid. She does not want to be told that she's too old to pull another man, or that her fashion sense is nonexistent and she dresses like a tart. He does not want to know she slept with his best mate when he went on a business trip to Germany, or that he is lousy at sex.

This is losing control — not keeping it

SPENDING HOLIDAYS ALONE

If there one thing that will bring about an overwhelming sense of loneliness, it's the prospect of spending the holidays alone. Bank holidays can be a nightmare if you've always spent them with your partner and children. Christmas and the New Year in particular can be spent in a wallow of alcoholic self-pity is you're not careful, so a bit of forward planning is essential

As part of the divorce proceedings, the court will try to encourage a fair and sensible arrangement when it comes to sharing the children's company at holiday time. Whatever your domestic circumstances and the permutations of holiday schedules, one of you will finish up spending holidays alone. Added to this, whenever you get a divorce there will be a holiday just around the corner and although finances will play a large part in what you can realistically afford, try to arrange a diversion.

Parent With Care Alone

If you are prepared to be reasonable there are going to be times when you are not going to have your children's company at the key holiday points – Christmas and/or New Year and Easter. One mother of our acquaintance arranges a special Christmas Eve supper for her two children and following the Christmas morning present opening, hands them over to their father before flying out to Spain for a week with a friend. Both parents have the pleasure of Christmas morning with their children having worked out a healthy compromise.

There *are* parents who have managed to work things out to a mutually convenient rota but, more often than not, the parent with care either makes visiting difficult for the ex-; or the absent parent makes no effort to see the children, especially when there's a new romance in the offing.

Whatever you decide to do, don't sit brooding while your children are with their mother/father. Use the time to your best advantage and do something you want to do and rarely found time for – visit friends you haven't seen for a while and stop over. Book into a health club and enjoy being pampered.

It takes time to adjust to being 'child-less' but it does have its advantages if you and your ex- can synchronise your activities. This system worked with pets, too!

Absent Parent Alone

For the absent parent, often things are much grimmer – particularly if they've lost both home and children in a divorce settlement and, if forced to live in rented accommodation, there may not been the facilities to entertain children. Absent parents can spend a lot of time chasing around the countryside, especially if their ex- has moved away and it means a long journey in order to visit. In a lot of instances, the cost is prohibitive and the absent parent cannot afford the travel costs and/or overnight accommodation on a regular basis.

Unless the absent parent has family or friends who are willing to include them and the children at holiday time, it may be difficult not to appear mean or second-rate in comparison to what they might expect at home. Maintaining contact is the important thing.

One absent father got around the distance problem by giving his daughter a pay-as-you-go mobile phone which meant they could both keep in touch despite the fact that the girl's mother always tried to obstruct them by arranging some conflicting event at holiday times. New legislation, however, will shortly be introduced to give the courts the right to require mothers to repay costs to fathers if they change arrangements at the last minute. For example, the mother could be forced to pay for a holiday the father had booked if she refused to let the child go. She could also have to pay his travel costs if she stopped him seeing the children when he arrived to take them out.

Let's face it, the absent parent spends a lot of time without the children and so needs to make a more concerted effort to arrange *personal* holiday plans. It may be that you were forced to give up some leisure or sporting activity when you got married – well, now's the time to resurrect that interest. There may be places to go, or things you've always wanted to do, and now you have the opportunity to take up fell walking, or visit museums and art galleries. It's time to start on a new path in life when you can turn holidays to your own advantage.

ASKING FOR HELP

One thing to remember is: don't ever feel that being unable to cope is a sign of weakness. Whether you're the one struggling to bring up the children; or whether the divorce has left you lonely and financially embarrassed, there are organisations that can offer help. It may just be someone to talk to — or you may need practical help in solving certain problems that have arisen as a result of the divorce. Divorce leaves an enormous gap in the lives of those involved and it's not always the 'guilty' party who suffers most.

Feeling unable to cope:

Reason why you may not feel you can cope:

- Unable to move on from your old life and 'let go' ☑
- Unresolved conflicts with a member of the family ☑
- You have debts that need to be paid off ☒
- Insufficient funds to meet your obligations ☒
- An overwhelming feeling of loneliness and isolation ☑
- Your emotional and/or physical health is suffering ☑
- Unable to juggle the children and a full-time job ☑
- Living in a unsatisfactory environment ☒
- A lack of friendship and/or social life ☒
- There seems little point in carrying on ☑

These are only a few of the reasons why the world can be a very bleak place for those coming to terms with divorce. These can usually be broken down into financial or emotional problems. Those marked with ☑ are emotional difficulties that can be resolved with a little bit of help from trained counsellors, family or friends. Those marked ☒ have their roots in a basic lack of finances and may need professional advice. As you can see the problems are pretty evenly divided with a 6/4 swing in the emotion stakes.

When we are hurting emotionally it is extremely difficult to function properly on any sort of level and unless we get to grips with the situation, things are unlikely to improve. If there seems little point in carrying on now that we're on our own, we're hardly likely to be in the right frame of mind to sort out our financial difficulties. Trying to juggle children and a full-time job leaves no time for personal space and so the overwhelming feeling of loneliness is compounded by the lack of time for a social life.   A lack of funds makes it impossible to get out of the rut if you can't even afford the price of a pint at the local pub. Unresolved conflicts with the family means there are less people around to give us a helping hand, or an invitation to supper.

CHILD SUPPORT AGENCY

Finally, if there was ever a Sword of Damocles hanging over divorcing parents, it must be the thousands of horror stories relating to the Child Support Agency (CSA) and the misery that this system has caused. Nearly everyone in the country has a "friend who got done by the CSA" and so the myth is self-perpetuating. Especially when the media report on the latest suicide, or a second family forced to split up because of exorbitant child maintenance payments to the first wife. Not forgetting the total disregard of lump-sum payments and fresh claims for maintenance by an ex- when they've found themselves short of cash, or dumped by the new boyfriend.

If divorces involving children are conducted properly through the court, it is possible to mutually agree the amount of child maintenance together with all other financial matters, by drawing up a Consent Order. Finances, including child maintenance can always be settled out of court but it is imperative that they be placed in the proper Consent Order documentation to be stamped by the court. Once the court stamps the documents they are legal and binding for both parties. Failure to obtain a stamped Consent Order can lead to horrendous difficulties at a later date by one of you reneging on the agreement.

Changes to the law

There has, however, been some insidious new changes made to the law came into effect in April 2002. By simplifying the formula, this new legislation means that an absent parent will be paying 15% of their net income for one child; 20% for two children and for three or more children, 25%. Under the former scheme the cost of the absent parent's accommodation was taken into account but the new laws scrapped that, and absent parents are now finding themselves with a non-negotiable increase in maintenance payments for amounts they cannot afford. Unfairly, it seems, the income of the parent with care is *not* taken into account.

The changes also gave the CSA the power to strip non-payers of their driving licenses as a punishment but this had only been implemented in two cases during the first 24 months after the Government introduced the penalty.

Agreeing maintenance

It is obviously in the interest of the absent parent to agree the amount of maintenance through a Court Order, which means that the CSA will not be involved unless the parent with care goes on Income Support. No matter how well you and your ex- get on, *do not make an informal agreement* when it comes to child maintenance.

Under the new rules things will not be so easy. In the future, even if you and your ex- agree on a sum and the court confirms that agreement in an Order, after one year, either party may go back to the CSA and request an amendment. This only applies to orders made after the Act came into affect and if you are receiving child maintenance under an existing Court Order, you will not be directly affected by the new legislation.

Make sure you are fully conversant with the rules governing the CSA and maintenance payments, because there are some extremely nasty clauses lurking in the shadows, especially with regard to an absent parent and a new partner. This is an area where all the facts should be made known to your solicitor at the time of the divorce ... not 12 months down the line when your ex- decides to move the goalposts because her new relationship has gone pear-shaped and she's short of cash.

VIEWPOINTS FROM THE LAYMAN'S ARMS

Marion and Gerald had been married for over 25 years having met at university. Gerald went into law, Marion stayed at home and had the three children who totally took over her life. Whenever Gerald suggested she accompany him socially, she was always too tired, or one of the children needed her to do something else. Eventually he stopped asking her and went alone. Finally, aged 56, he met Barbara whom he wanted to marry. Marion was furious and slashed all his suits, maintaining that after all she'd done for him, she was entitled to the family home and maintenance, even though all the children had left full time education. "I didn't want to spend the rest of my life watching her knitting," said Gerald. "I had a last chance of happiness and I was damned well going to take it." He offered Marion a small elegant town-house and a regular allowance which she has refused. She also encourages their youngest son not to work so that he remains at home and a dependant.. Should Marion be allowed to penalise Gerald when she had obviously lost interest in him as a husband many years before?

Male opinion

"Gerald tried to involve his wife in his social life; she was not willing or interested. No fault of his for what happened. She should settle for the offer, if not, then hard lines, Marion!"

"Since he's obviously picked up the tabs and never got anything back for it, I hope the court forces the sale of the property. It will teach his grasping son a lesson at the same time."

Female opinion

"It sounds as though Marion married for security. She has been boring and selfish and I think Gerald's offer was more than fair. She isn't entitled to any more than a smaller house and an allowance."

"He's being more than fair. She didn't want him, so why not let him go and have the luxury of independence?"

"Divorced couples hob-nobbed with each, and with each other's correspondents."

[Noel Coward, *Present Indicative*]

Chapter Five

The Judgement of Solomon

When it comes to divorce and the children, the question of financial settlements will be handled by the court which, as we have seen, will put the interests of the children before everything else. When it comes to dividing a couple's assets on a more personal basis, however, there can be no hard and fast rules as to who gets what. Here we are looking at possessions that have sentimental rather than monetary value and a certain amount of give and take must be entered into where possible.

THE FINANCIAL REALITY

If your grandmother gave you that nice little Renoir for the bedroom don't think for one moment that this will escape the notice of the avaricious partner who is out for all they can get. The fact that it is a family heirloom will cut no ice. Personal and family jewellery may even suffer the same fate, so it's a good idea if you can both behave sensibly and you might *both* come out reasonable satisfied with the division.

Over the years, Graham's mother had given Lucy a considerable amount of family antiques for their home but when it came to the divorce, Lucy maintained that her mother-in-law had given everything to her personally. Graham said that as they were family pieces he'd actually like to keep some of them for himself and was willing to negotiate. Unexpectedly, Lucy booked a removal van while Graham was at work and took everything with her, leaving him with a virtually empty house. "I could have cheerfully broken her neck," he said bitterly. "None of those things could be replaced and all had memories of my childhood home. All she cared about was the possession."

When Sue and Arnold divorced, his mother sent round a typewritten inventory of all the things she'd given them for the home and asked for them back. "I wasn't that keen on the stuff myself," said Sue, "and as far as I was concerned she could have had the lot but her attitude pissed me off so much that I sold the lot to a second-hand dealer and sent her the money. Yes, it was petty but we never liked each other and so I didn't feel the need to be pleasant."

Do remember that sentimental attachment doesn't necessarily mean an item is valuable. One couple came to their most acrimonious wrangling over their record collection; another couple almost came to blows when the wife gave her husband's collection of beer mats to a nephew!

SPLITTING UP THE HOME

If the court rules that the existing family home is to be maintained for the children until they finish their education, it may well include the existing contents. This means that the husband or wife moving out may have to leave virtually everything behind which is deemed necessary for the children. Needless to say, this is where a great deal of animosity is generated.

Where a decision has been made to split up the home it is best left to the discretion of the parties involved. It is impractical to fight out content claims in court since in most cases the costs would exceed the value of the contents (unless the family Rembrandt is being called into question). "Allow a degree of generosity," advises one leading divorce lawyer, "make the grand gesture ..." The following guidelines may help to arrive at an amicable solution:

- Each should have his or her own *personal* clothes and belongings

- If individual items were owned by either of you before you were married, or were given to you individually by your family or friends, it is realistic that you should have these things if you want them.

- If items are duplicated (and unless dividing them up destroys a major part of the value) it is reasonable that each of you should have a choice of the duplicated items.

- Everything else should be divided equally, but if you cannot agree prepare a list of the items in dispute or those of value, and take it in turns to make a selection from the list. Throw a coin to see who has first choice off the list.

- If you own a car, this should remain with the one who needs it for work. If you have two cars, each should stick with the one he or she mostly uses.

The court can order that everything be sold so that the cash can be divided but this is impractical since it entails a massive loss of resources for the family. Do try, however, to maintain a sense of proportion when it comes to dividing up the household.

When Gerald and Rose split up, he methodically when through everything to make sure that the items were divided fairly. "It started off like a French farce," remembers Rose, "but it rapidly deteriorated into anger. He was splitting up glass and china so that we landed up with three plates, cups and saucers each from one set and a further three items from another, instead of having a complete set each. We each finished up with a collection that looked like a job-lot from the auction rooms so I finally told him where to stick it. He was most offended because he thought he was being generous and fair!"

WHO GETS THE DOG?

It's not just humans who get upset, confused and displaced by divorce, the family pet is just as likely to find itself left out in the cold. According to The Blue Cross, a large number of pets, mostly cats and dogs, find themselves unwanted when a relationship breaks down. "Divorce is a common reason why pets finish up at

The Blue Cross," said Communications Officer, Yvonne Lilley. "People are moving to smaller homes and often do not want to have the added responsibility on top of everything else."

The Blue Cross has four hospitals and 12 Adoption Centres which act as receiving points for unwanted pets but it is difficult to assess just how many dogs and cats are casualties of divorce. "People are often embarrassed to admit they have to get rid of a pet because their relationship has failed and they simply can't cope. We take in a quite a high proportion from people who do admit to being in this position but it doesn't account for those animals that are simply abandoned or left tied to a post outside a Centre."

Fortunately, the majority owners wouldn't dream of abandoning their pets and many have spent thousands of pounds in legal costs to do battle in court over who gets the cat or dog. In fact, there have been numerous cases of this nature but be warned, judges take a dim view over this sort of behaviour.

By rule of thumb, animal should be with the person who can best take care of their needs, and the welfare of the dog or cat should be paramount, regardless of legal ownership. A large dog, used to regular walks and a large garden, cooped up in a flat is bound to become bored and develop serious behavioural problems as a result. In many cases, the lease on a flat will expressly forbid the keeping of animals on the property, so the pet's needs must be taken into consideration in the early stages of divorce, not as an after-thought.

"When we were splitting up, my ex- announced that he wanted to take his cat, the elder of our two pedigrees, to live in a flat," said Gabrielle. "I knew he was only being difficult and didn't really want the cat, so I said 'Fine, take him'. For the next week I couldn't look the cat in the face because I felt so guilty but I knew that if I'd said anything else, my ex- *would* have taken the cat to spite me.

"I devised a campaign whereby I casually discussed the cost of special diet cat food, the need for regular flea treatment, vet's bills for an aging and incontinent cat, not to mention the fact that a pet insurance company wouldn't touch an elderly cat. The incontinence manifested on the kitchen floor at regular intervals in the form of carefully collected cat turds from the litter tray and weak orange squash poured onto newspaper to give that fetching 'stale urine look'. After a further week my ex- announced that he didn't think it would be fair to take the cat and keep him shut up in a flat all day while he was at work - and would I take him."

When Sheila and Eric parted, she decided that it was better for her Labrador to be left at the farm where it was used to running about all day with the rest of the farm dogs. "I was moving to a small cottage with hardly any garden, and working full-time. It broke my heart but it wouldn't have been fair to take her away."

Sometimes, a dog seems like the only friend you've got left. "I couldn't have faced the bleakness leading up to the divorce if I hadn't had my big old dog," said Patricia, "and he's been there for me through all the bad times. Those furry shoulders had a lot of crying done on them, I can tell you."

Richard used to spend a lot of time talking to his dog following the divorce. "He acted as a sounded board for how I was feeling at the time."

There are all sorts of problems to face when moving the family pets. Sometimes it might be better to either put the dog into kennels or have a friend dog-sit while your move is in progress. Dogs enjoy the thrill of new places although they are just as susceptible to upset while adjusting to changes within the household. Make sure it doesn't get caught up with the excitement of all the activity and run off while the furniture removers are in and out of the house — both at your old address and the new one. If you are moving some distance away, it may be better to find a kennels near your new home and leave the dog with them until you've moved in. Don't forget an up-to-date certificate of vaccination will be required.

Cats will always present much more of a problem since it will be necessary to keep them shut in the new house for at least two days. Select one of the rooms that can be shut off with food, water, a litter tray and a basket, cushion or chair that has a familiar smell. At the end of the day when everyone is in for the night, let the cat out, making sure that no doors or windows have been left open. Try to keep the cat inside for 48 hours before letting it out, and then only do this just before feeding time. Cats are sensitive creatures and may need a medicinal tin of pilchards or tuna to convince them that life is worth living after all.

Small caged birds and other small pets such as mice, guinea pigs, hamsters and rabbits should be transported in secure, draught-proof containers. Remove all toys but make sure that they have access to food and water in non-spill containers because it's quite easy to overlook their needs during the chaos of moving.

SHARED BUSINESS INTERESTS

If a husband and wife are in business together it is obvious that a divorce will have serious repercussions on their working relationship. Many family businesses are acquired through inheritance and the one leaving cannot automatically expect a share in the value of the business that will bankrupt it. In the instance when a family's livelihood is derived from the business alone, often one partner is the mainstay while the other is involved to a much lesser degree, and any financial provision that can be made will depend on what the business can afford.

In the case of a professional set-up that is dependent upon professional qualifications or specialist experience, the business can only survive if the one with the relevant qualification/experience continues to run it. In many cases the history and nature of the business interests may govern who continues to operate it — although in an ideal world if the couple are able, a new partnership agreement could be drawn up to enable them to continue to work together even if the marriage has failed.

If the business is to continue, the following should be taken into account:

1. If the business came from the family of the husband or wife, usually that person keeps the business

2. The business stays with the one who has been responsible for running it, particularly if their professional expertise makes him or her the one who can realistically do so

3. If the business can be divided and both husband and wife have been equally responsible for the day to day running of it, then a sensible and fair division of the assets could be the solution

4. If both parties find they are able to continue to work together then the business can carry on as before

So what share of a continuing business may one partner of the marriage expect if the business and its value are to stay with the other? Obviously, however, arrangements as complicated as this can only be arrived at by prior negotiation between the couple – and the help of a solicitor. As a going concern the business may be very valuable, but that value often exists only on paper unless, or until it is sold. In the past the courts have ruled that whatever the family business may be worth on paper, an outgoing martial partner can 'only expect to receive such a sum as the business can reasonably raise without imperilling its future existence' (*Spitting Up* – David Green).

Understanding new laws
The new laws governing the division of assets may have an adverse effect on what is considered 'a share of the business'. As a solicitor commented wryly when the House of Lords ruling was announced: "Lawyers and accountants will be coming up with some innovative proposals as to how the financial arrangements can be re-arranged

to suit their clients.' Then there was Lord Justice Thorpe's explanation of why fair division assets did not necessarily require equal shares since the court should recognise 'the product of the genius with which only one of the spouses may be endowed'.

How this is supposed to work in practical terms has still not been explained, and is largely depended on how judges interpret the rulings and the outcome of current cases. Just remember that the more you wrangle over a settlement, the higher the legal fees and the less you'll *both* have at the end if you go for annihilation of the golden goose for purely selfish motives.

FRIENDS & ENEMIES

No matter how well we think we get on with our friends, they will invariably fall into 'his' and 'hers' when it comes to divorce. It's a phenomena that is written and talked about but no one seems to be able to explain why those whom we looked upon as good and trusted friends are conspicuous by their absence once the *decree absolute* has been made?

Everyone warns us that this will happen but we never believe it - until we find ourselves alone with a Saturday night bottle of Chardonnay and a supper for one. There appears no logical explanation why this occurs. One minute we're invited round for meals following an after-work session at the gym: the next we're ostracised and wracking our brains for something that we may have done or said that has given offence.

Let's put the cards on the table. Once divorced, whether male or female, you become *dangerous*! Yes, really ... as in predatory. The fact that you've always been on huggy-kissy terms with Angela is irrelevant. John noticed that extra long squeeze (which was meant to convey how much you've appreciated their kindness), and decided you'd got the hots for his wife.

Janice's coolness the last time you went to the theatre might stem from the innocent comment you made about how lucky she was to be married to Robert, and she's decided you've got the hots for her husband.

Predatory urges also seem to work the other way. "Why is it always your ex-husband's best friend who's sliding his hand up your knicker-leg before the ink's dry on the *decree absolute*?" asked Carol.

Martin was horrified when his ex-wife's best friend turned up with a bottle of champagne and announced that they were going to celebrate his divorce by going to bed together. "She claimed she's always fancied me and now that Polly was out of the way, we didn't need to worry. I know she'd always been a bit of a 'goer' but she'd never tried it on with me before. She frightened me to death."

The message is that as you are used to being married (i.e. having regular sex), you must be missing it and will do anything to get laid! That's why you are dangerous.

Sue who's been both divorcee and widow says she'll go for the latter every time. "Both male and female friends seem to look upon the newly divorced state as a frenetic round of lemming-like sexual activity. Widowhood, on the other hand, extracts dignified respect and sympathy. Given the choice I'd always go for death, it's so much more *reassuring*, some how — and less expensive."

There will, of course, always be that hard-core who will back you whether you've taken up professional lap-dancing, or been arrested for the assassination of Kennedy (President, that is, not Nigel). This hard-core, however, will not share that allegiance with both parties — last one in, first one out and all that — so spare them the embarrassment of having to refuse your invitations if you attempt to maintain a friendship with your ex's staunch chums. It's time to move on ...

IT'S DIFFERENTFOR MEN

Although *Men Are From Mars, Women Are From Venus* (John Gray) went a long way in explaining the differences between the emotional reactions of the 'different' species, there is very little allowances made for these differences on a social level. Men *do* react differently to women, especially when it comes to communicating and despite the fact that millions of column inches have been devoted to the emergence of 'the New Man', the majority of males still retain those chauvinistic tendencies that women seem to find so difficult to deal with.

Few men are like Dennis Quaid, who could talk openly about his feelings when he broke up with his wife, Meg Ryan. "When you break up your whole identity is shattered. That's why it's like death ... Next to losing a child, the break-up of a marriage is the hardest thing to go through. You can stop talking to each other and pretend it never happened — that's the way it would have been if we didn't have a child together. Things happen. It doesn't mean that people are bad people."

Under any normal circumstances, however, men do not confide in others. Neither do they pour over weekly magazines, subconsciously planning their strategy from articles, books, television and friends' conversations in order to prepare for the inevitable collapse of the marriage. Men do not seek a divorce for what they would consider 'trivial' reasons despite the fact that a series of 'compound issues' (see Chapter One) can seriously undermine a couple's relationship. Men prefer to grapple with tangible problems, which is why they are so often totally baffled by what they see as a woman's histrionics over something quite unimportant.

Vanessa Lloyd Platt has observed a new trend developing over the last five years, whereby men from all walks of life are complaining about what they see as 'uncontrolled aggression' in their wives' behaviour. "Too often, in divorce proceedings, I observe the Dragon Woman," she writes in *Secrets of Successful Relationships*, "whose conduct is bound to exterminate any relationship in which she is involved, and the counterpart she has created, Colditz Man, who cannot wait to plot his escape from her." According to Ms

Lloyd Platt's clients, women seem to be turning the home-front into a battle zone and the men are running for cover.

Man Talk

To carry the military analogy still further, the first edition of this book featured *The Married Men's Militia,* an Internet support organisation dealing with divorce, custody and settlement issues and although it was aimed at the American legal system, it contained some good old-fashioned 'corn an' grits' home truths. As the 'Colonel' explained: "Just cause it's funny, don't mean we ain't serious! The M3 Battlesite is not for the faint hearted or politically-correct wussies who can't appreciate man-talk."

The Colonel's seven buddies were all divorce-veterans who 'traded drinks for advice' and subsequently, having seen 'some serious divorce campaigning' decided to set up their website for the benefit of others. At the time there was nothing quite like it in the UK and the style was completely '*Platoon* with attitude', but there was a poignancy in the words that may have struck the right note with men who felt there was nowhere to turn, or that no one understood how they were feeling.

In true bar-talk jargon they discussed feeling a sense of loss of control and hope. "Your family life will seem separate from your life, almost like it belonged to some other poor bozo. Family life will have taken on a life of its own and it won't be your life. Or what you want your life to be. You may even discover that neighbours or the hardware store lady seem to know more about what's happening with your wife and kids than you do. Those feelings that it will all work out okay will have disappeared long ago. You won't be able to imagine the rest of your life being like it's been the last year without wanting to reach for a bottle or a 12 gauge - but that may just seem like too much trouble.

"You won't stop loving anybody. But you'll know you aren't in love with your wife any more. When she walks by you naked on her way to the bathroom, or says she's taking in a movie with her girlfriends, or says she's sending the kids to camp, it'll be about as important to you as some movie you saw once that had the same thing in it and now can't remember the movie's name. And you don't care to."

Since then, the UK has seen the growth of its own new civil rights movement, Fathers 4 Justice, that campaigns for a child's rights to see both parents and grandparents. Adopting a twin track strategy, based on self-publicity and good press, they have attracted a lot of public sympathy with their high-profile Batman and Robin,, and Spiderman campaigns.

Recognising expectations

It should also be a recognised fact that men do not have the advantage of being 'conditioned' by the media into accepting the foregone conclusion that they *will* eventually end up in the divorce court.

Look at all the women's magazines and you will see a common theme running through them. From a very young target market it is possible to trace the constant barrage of subliminal messaging that alerts the female of the species to the shortcomings in her men. From their early teens, girls are informed that men will let them down; will chat up their best friends and sleep with the hired help; or cannot be trained to do simple household chores from washing up to producing the perfect orgasm.

When the marriage inevitably hits a bad patch, there's more back-up material to convince her why it is a good idea to dump him — the magazine 'experts' say it's okay!

Under the circumstances it is not surprising that men tend to feel more isolated during divorce for the simple reason that they often have no one to talk to about events as they happen. Few women have difficulty in discussing the most intimate details with their friends or counsellor, but men are more reticent about things that trouble them.

This means that when a man stubbornly continues to watch the cricket match on television when you want to discuss divorce proceedings, he may just be trying to conceal his hurt.

THE CLOCK IS RUNNING

The sands of time trickle through slowly enough when we're in our twenties but as the years pass many of us are forced to view our circumstances with an eye on the future. People often register the passage of time for different reasons. For the wanna-be divorcee, it's a question of synchronising career and assets *v.* future and life-style. It's often a time for looking at a partner and deciding whether you wish to remain with them or try for something better.

A harsh judgement perhaps, but more people dump their part-ner because they wish to improve themselves than they'd like to admit. In these post-millennium days of expanding learning oppor-tunities, no one needs to remain in the job they started when they left full-time schooling. Career changes are open to all and anyone has the opportunity to obtain a degree or educational certificate of some kind if they put their mind to it. How many of those 160,000+ divorces are the result of one partner deciding that the other is 'holding them back' once they've discovered a new talent for themselves which they feel they want to develop unhindered by a relationship that has gone stale?

THIRTY ...

Being single again in your thirties may not be all it's cracked up to be: the competition is tougher, for a start. This is the age grouping identified as 'Thatcher's children', i.e. those who were born during the seventies into an "I want it all and can have it all" society. If we're looking for romance, another relationship or marriage, the prospects might not be as rosy as we thought back behind the marital barricades.

The popularity of the *Bridget Jones* boom has revealed what columnist Minette Marrin described as a 'very sad contemporary phenomenon — the superfluous 30-something woman'.

In a conversation with a colleague, Ms Marrin was asked: "What has a fading, work-obsessed, sub-fertile neurotic 30-something got to offer the sort of man she's looking for? Especially when she'd probably dump him and remove his children and half his assets anyway?" Marrin reports that two very young women who were listening were shocked and offended, but they could offer no positive response.

Thirty-somethings are ambitious, not just in their careers but also when it comes to settling down and raising a family. Women are far choosier than men but it is still apparent that they're not really prepared to do without the 'ideal of high romance' either. There is also some indication that 30-something men are turning towards younger or *older* women, leaving 'quite a lot of superfluous thirty-something women, washed up on the banks of time's ever-flowing stream' observes Marrin.

Being Realistic

So, if you're thinking of trading in your own thirty-something partner for a more dynamic and ambitious model, you may have to think again. On the other hand, if you have a successful career and feel that you will cope perfectly well living on your own, then the world could well be your oyster. Financially, you may experience a slight setback but there's still a long way to go ... and if you're going to be paying for your children until they finish full-time education this might be another sound reason for thinking again.

Is it your partner who is at fault?

Or is it you?

FORTY ...

Since the average age for divorce is 40 for men and 38 for women and men are more likely to remarry than women, it would appear that the odds are levelling out. It also means that a highly successful career can be used to finance a divorce if one partner (who also gets care of the children) decides to call it a day. Forty-somethings also seem to find the allure of art and religion, particularly alternative religion, a fascination.

 When James was divorced he decided to enrol at Art College. "I'd always wanted to go and once I was on my own again, there was nothing stopping me. My year was made up of predominantly 40-something women who all wanted to find themselves and 'the goddess within'. Most of them were anti-male, dressed like 60s hippies but with short-cropped hair.

"One in particular was in her late forties and was quite open about the fact that when she'd got through College (which was being financed by her husband), she intended to leave him. The subject for her first year piece was entitled 'She' and involved a female friend from the photographic class taking pictures of her genitalia that she would then transpose into a series of sculptured images. What her family thought about their mother's fanny plastered all over the walls of the exhibition, I really can't imagine."

Mel, a spiritual mentor with Pathfinders, confirms that 40-something is a common age for women to find religion. "Unfortunately, they develop an almost missionary-like zeal and a frighteningly violent reaction to anyone who doesn't conform to their own brand of feminist-goddess-vegetarianism. They talk constantly about finding themselves but rarely pay anyone else the courtesy of listening to their viewpoint – especially if it happens to be male.

"Needless to say, there is a high proportion of marriage break-ups as a result of this involvement and you can hardly blame the husbands for being glad to see the back of them. This isn't just alternative religions, certain Christian sects also have to take their fair share of the blame."

On the marital front, forty-something appears to be a great time of upheaval and changes in personal direction. Just be sure that what you are looking for isn't an illusion.

FIFTY ...

Finding ourselves involved in a marital upheaval when we've reached the 50 mark, however, is a much bigger shock and less easier to cope with than when we're in our thirties or even forties. A large number of divorced people in this age group have never made any long-term savings for themselves because they assumed they would be adequately provided for in retirement and that their marriages would last.

Fifty is not a good time of your life to find yourself forced to take charge of your own financial affairs. Many wives still rely on their husbands to take care of the finances and a large number of husbands don't have a clue when it comes to home economics. On the plus side, divorcees of 50+ are usually looking at a higher cash settlement because, more often than not, the house has been paid for and the children have finished full-time education. This means that the property can be sold to give both sufficient capital to buy something smaller, but it will also mean that both scrape the bottom of the savings barrel.

There are an increasing number of 50-something women who now earn more than their husbands, which means that there is no retirement provision from the divorce. Finding yourself on your own again at 50, with only ten years to go to retirement, is a daunting prospect for both men and women.

"My ex- kindly informed me that I didn't stand a chance of meeting anyone else now that I'd hit fifty," said Claire. "Men can always attract younger women but at fifty you've had it, he added." As it happened, Claire met Alex shortly after the divorce was finalised. She joined a local group for mature 'singles' and enjoys a highly active social life with her new man friend.

There are a growing number of activities for the 'grey army' and with just a little bit of effort, you can find yourself never short of company, or something to do. Men are now starting to be in short supply and so for the first time, the *chaps* are in a position to pick and choose.

VIEWPOINTS FROM THE LAYMAN'S ARMS

George was a high-powered oil engineer whose job took him all over the world. When he was aged 43 his wife announced she wanted a divorce and the court awarded her the house and a settlement for the two children. Because he'd been a high earner they'd managed to purchase a large property and George's suggestion that they sell it and each buy a smaller house was met with refusal. The high mortgage payments and the stress of the divorce made him ill and the next thing he knew, the CSA was harrying him, which subsequently led to a complete nervous breakdown.

He was homeless and without a job, until a friend offered him a position as live-in gardener and chauffer. He now has a roof over his head and lives off the produce he grows in the garden with 'a few bob over for one or two luxuries' but he will never go back to his old high-flying days in the oil industry. He doesn't have any contact with his former family who have been forced to leave their home due to him defaulting on the mortgage and hold him responsible. Should he have been expected to maintain a highly expensive house even though his income made it possible at the time of the divorce?

Male opinion:

"Why is it that the man is the one to be penalised in circumstances such as these? His idea of them each having a smaller house was ideal, but again greed entered the room and cost him everything, even his health. I think it's time changes were made in the handling of such cases."

"With a family like that you don't need enemies. Okay, legally he should provide for his kids, but they've obviously not bothered to provide for him when he was ill. This is where the court should have forced the house sale and allowed everyone to walk away with something. Having said that, they'd probably have kept asking for more — even after a court ruling."

Female opinion:

"Poor George! His original suggestion was sensible and would have kept both parties in an acceptable style. Her greed has ruined both their lives. He should stop earning anything for a couple of years — then disappear and start again under a new name. Leave them to fend for themselves!"

"I hope his family are enjoying their new home! Wherever it is."

Chapter Six

Dealing With Difficult Partners

The most difficult aspect of being married to a violent partner is the inability to talk about it, or to galvanise yourself into taking any action. Women have a marked reluctance to admit, even to themselves, that the situation is *not* going to get better, while men feel that it's too humiliating to confess they are being knocked around by their wives. Nevertheless domestic violence is a growing problem and, although in many instances the violence may not have actually erupted into a physical assault, the implied threat hangs there like an assassin's blade.

VIOLENT PARTNERS

Most couples fight - some even throw things and resort to pushing and shoving - but real domestic violence is a nightmare for anyone trapped in its snare. Up to a few years ago, it was dismissed as a working class phenomena but research has shown that domestic violence permeates all levels of society. Regardless of background, parents who hit their children programme into their children's brains a tendency to physical aggression.

The problem is self-perpetuating as once aggression is established in the brain it can become part of the individual's *natural* reaction to situations. Children in nursery school who display aggression are more than likely to develop into aggressive teenagers and adults. On study showed that both boys and girls who were remembered by their classmates as being particularly aggressive when they were eight years old were the ones who were the most aggressive when they were 30-year old adults. As adults they were more than likely to be violent towards their marriage partner.

One of the main problems is that aggression can often pay off. It can be a rather useful way of getting on in the world and many aggressive, violent people have no desire to overcome it because it gives them a measure of control over people and circumstances. Many of those who have suffered at the hands of a violent partner often received their first beating within months or even weeks of their marriage.

According to a consultant forensic psychiatrist, there are five distinct categories of men who are violent towards their wives:

⇒ dependent, passive men who suddenly 'lose it' under direct provocation from a domineering wife.

⇒ suspicious types who are jealous of their wives, usually without grounds.

⇒ dominant men who still need to prove themselves

⇒ bullies

⇒ average husbands who suffer periods of severe mental disturbance

The reactions within these categories can vary tremendously but are usually activated by three identifiable triggers:

⇒ the need to control or punish
⇒ aggressive squabbling
⇒ alcohol

Despite the fact that most books and magazine articles are written on the subject of male behaviour, it's also an urban myth that *all* domestic violence is the province of the male of the species. Women may often lack the physical strength but they can be equally as handy with their fists or a weapon if they are convinced that a man will not retaliate.

Solicitors are reporting a marked increase in the number of men who admit to being psychically assaulted by their wives on a regular basis, but, so far, very little has been written on the subject on which to base any psychological reasoning for this behaviour.

SO WHY DON'T YOU LEAVE?

Because it's easier said than done. As Lucy pointed out, "Being married to a violent partner is so exhausting, both emotionally and physically, that you don't have the energy to do anything about the problem. You're too busy mentally ducking and diving in order not to invite another pasting."

Corrective violence is the most dangerous type of all — and a lot more common that many people would like to imagine. Although ostensibly identified as a need to control or punish, it is often accompanied by numerous other abusive tactics that would beggar belief as the victim is toyed with like a mouse at the mercy of a cat. Victims of this sort of behaviour will admit that more often than not it was the *verbal* abuse, coupled with the emotional and psychological bullying, that took its toll. Having been cut off from their friends and family (often by a move to a new location) the perpetrator assumes total control and the undermining of their partner's self-confidence begins.

What appears even more incomprehensible to an outsider, is that those who find themselves in situations like this, are usually highly intelligent people. Even the most intelligent of people, however, will eventually come to believe that they are stupid, unattractive, dull and useless under a constant barrage of threats and criticism. Added to this there is the deliberately contrived lack of resources — money, clothes, car — needed to make a clean getaway. This kind of control ensures that the victim will never have the confidence or strength to walk out, and so the violence continues until something drastic happens.

BREAKING THE TIES

Aggressive squabbling and alcohol-related violence can often be triggered by stress and if your partner is willing to seek help in order to try to work out your difficulties, there may still be a chance that your marriage can be saved. If not, then you need to seriously consider seeking the advice of a solicitor. Because of the emotional issues involved, you may find it easier to make a written record of

your complaint (which you'll have to do sooner or later). This will:
a) avoid a tearful break-down in front of the solicitor
b) save time
c) lessen the embarrassment

When discussing violent behaviour it is very easy to leave love out of the equation but many women who find themselves a victim of domestic violence will admit to still being in love with their partner. Many convince themselves that they still stand a chance of changing an aggressor; or that the violent attacks are their own fault.

A solicitor or Citizen's Advice Bureau can point you in the right direction when you finally decide enough is enough. The non-judgemental listening ear of an independent 'expert', who has heard it all before, may just be that small bit of support you've needed in order to make the break.

PROTECTION

It is important to understand that both cohabitees *and* spouses, can claim temporary protection for their occupation of property from the magistrates of County Courts if they are at risk of violence from their partner. A court can grant an injunction or order excluding a violent partner from the property, even from a house which s/he owns, or of which s/he is a tenant.

If you are going down this road, you can also lodge a complaint at your local police station's Domestic Violence Unit and be registered as being 'at risk'. Until recently domestic violence was looked upon as a private issue and the police rarely took any action, especially as the victim usually refused to press charges. Since it has been recognised as an 'identifiable criminal offence', the police now have the power to arrest and imprison an offender. In cases of extreme violence, the court can order a 'power of arrest' to be attached to orders for injunctions, which allows the police to act without having to make a further application to the court.

Although a child has the right to maintain contact with a parent, even a violent one, this right will be respected unless it is not in the *child's* own interest. Contact has been refused in cases where there was a clear risk of violence between parent and child, especially in the event of mental illness.

Although most people is these situations show a marked reluctance to involve the authorities, it is essential that you act through a solicitor right from the beginning. No matter how much your family and friends are willing to help, it is unreasonable to expect them to put up with a violent and/or drunken spouse hammering on their door, demanding admittance.

CONTROL FREAKS & DRAMA QUEENS

In the majority of cases, the control freak or drama queen, doesn't inflict any actual *physical* violence, their form of control is much more insidious. The control freak gets his or her own way by manipulation and stealth, only becoming aggressive when their demands are not met. They are extremely exhausting and their partner creeps around, terrified that there will be sudden eruption to send children and pets scurrying for cover, while s/he receives a verbal dressing down. The partner on the receiving end of this treatment is permanently tired from trying to keep an immaculate house, spotless children and perfect garden under a constant barrage of criticism.

The drama queen is constantly seeking attention, ensuring that their impulsive or dramatic behaviour places them at the centre of things. They are prone to sulks and temper tantrums if they don't get their own way, even resorting to throwing things in the best theatrical manner. The partner of a drama queen is a nervous wreck because they don't know when the next outburst will manifest — or in what form. Both the control freak and the drama queen are exceeding shallow and are probably diagnosable as 'histrionic personalities'.

Remember that control freaks and drama queens can be of either sex, often exhibiting the following characteristics:

- Becoming bullying and aggressive if thwarted
- Throw tears and tantrums if thwarted

- Keep up a barrage of constant criticism
- Set unrealistically highly standards
- Constantly demand to be the centre of attraction
- Causes everyone to live in a permanent state of crisis

If you're happy to live life on a knife-edge of nervous twitching every time the door bangs, then fine ... but this will eventually takes its toll on your health and something has to give. Seek professional advice from organisations such as Relate, even if your partner refuses to accompany you since an independent view can help put things in perspective.

WHEN IT ALL ENDS IN TEARS

With violent relationships there is the *very* real threat that the aggression will be carried to such an extreme that it escalates completely out of control.

Lloyd and Frances:

Here we had an extremely attractive and popular couple who fought 'like cat and dog' almost from the start of their relationship. They had two small daughters and a hectic social life with a fast-moving crowd. Frances was possessive and if Lloyd were late home she would accuse him of all sorts of sexual misdemeanours, of which he was completely innocent. The fights were such that she frequently smashed a dinner plate or bottle and went for Lloyd with the broken shards in an attempt to disfigure him. He retaliated by hitting her. One evening things went too far. Lloyd strangled her and was sentenced to life imprisonment for murder.

Willis and Vanessa:

This was another highly volatile relationship that always stopped short of physical violence. One day, provoked into a rage whilst ironing, Vanessa tried to hit Willis full in the face with the hot iron. He grabbed her wrist and the iron fell against the glass door of the oven, smashing it. Angered still further by the broken glass,

Vanessa picked up the iron and went for him again, whereupon Willis hit her so hard that he broke her nose and front teeth. As a result, Willis was taken to court, divorced and has never seen his young son since, because he was considered to be a violent man — even though he'd never committed an act of violence against his wife before she attacked *him* with the iron.

Allan and Helen:

Much against her family's wishes, Helen married Allan when she became pregnant. Only weeks into the marriage she discovered that he became violent when he'd had too much to drink. Having thumped her several times while she was pregnant the first time, she nevertheless remained in love with him and two years later they had a second son. When the baby was three months old, Helen was subjected to a savage beating and left. They were divorced and although the contact was irregular there was always the old spark between them. They both went through a serious of relationships although Allan always maintained that he'd never found anyone he loved more than Helen. They'd been divorced over twenty years when he called unexpectedly to tell her that he'd met someone, was desperately in love and was going to marry her. His new lady-love felt there was something 'wrong' which she couldn't put her finger on and turned him down. A week later, Allan blew his brains out.

MEN BEHAVING BADLY

When relationships are over and the divorce court has passed its judgement over financial settlements and the children, men can often be left feeling resentful, especially if they weren't the one petitioning to end the marriage. While men can behave extremely badly *during* the divorce, once the *decree absolute* has been issued, most tend to knuckle down to re-building what's left of their lives.

This ability to pick themselves up, dust themselves off, etc., can, however, be seen as callous behaviour by their former partner.

"My ex is now resentful over the way I live my life as a single man," said Keith, "She's constantly carping about not having time to do anything other than look after the kids, the house and the garden. She tried to put me on a guilt trip by saying that I should help out for the kid's sake. Of course, I miss them and I see them whenever I can, but *she* threw me out because she needed more space for doing the things she wanted to do. I thought bugger it, you wanted the divorce, the house and the, kids, you sort it."

When one family split up, the husband carried on a high-profile legal battle over his three daughters after the divorce. The girls lived with their mother and both 'wanted and enjoyed' contact with their father until his antics led to him serving a 10-month sentence for contempt of court. Following a campaign of harassment in the form of demonstrations outside the homes of various judges, a High Court judge confirmed that all three daughters have ended up opposed to and refusing to participate in parental visits, having been left with a beleaguered feeling of being stalked and harassed.

In all fairness, many men *do* feel as though they've been handed a raw deal and very often resort to more childish forms of retaliation.

On the spur of the moment, Tim placed a card with his ex-wife's telephone number in a phone box, guessing that prostitutes advertising their wares left similar ones. His revenge only lasted as long as it took his ex- to change her phone number, but "I made me feel a hell of a lot better," he confessed.

Another made a point of sleeping with everyone of his former wife's friends — and telling her. "She'd accused me often enough of doing so, even though I never had. These were the same women who'd been encouraging her to get a divorce, so I just thought I'd make up for lost time and I was moving out of the area anyway. There was a lot of howling and recriminations after I'd left, I can tell you."

WOMEN BEHAVING BADLY

Love and hate are remarkably close to one another If we love someone, they have the power to hurt us by leaving us or humiliating us in some way. For women, they may come to hate their men in time honoured fashion: *Heaven has no rage like love to hatred turned, no hell a fury like a woman scorned.*

When Geraldine's husband went off to live with his mistress, his enraged wife tracked him down and poured paint stripper over the bonnet of his Bentley. Not only that, as he came roaring out of the entrance of the apartment building, she hit him straight in the genitals with a baseball bat! The ironic thing is that her behaviour convinced him just how much Geraldine loved him and he went back home — they've recently celebrated their 16th wedding anniversary despite standing by each other during serious health scares.

More and more frequently, high-profile court cases are showing that women are also demonstrating a much greater tendency to violence if thwarted in a relationship.

We have the case mentioned earlier where a wife of eighteen months tried to suffocate her husband because the marriage was obviously going wrong and she wanted to 'frighten him' into treating her better. It frightened him all right and, as a result, she was charged with attempted murder even though the jury acquitted her.

This was closely followed by the 'deadly revenge of jilted royal aide' who killed her lover by hitting him with a cricket bat and claiming that he "came on to" the knife she held for protection when he'd told her he no longer loved her and did not want to marry her. The prosecution offered that the woman was prompted by anger and vengeance, denying she had been jilted because she realised what a strong motive it was for murder. The jury returned a verdict of guilty and she was sentenced to life imprisonment.

COUNTING THE COST

Revenge may be sweet and a dish best tasted cold but for a warring couple, who are hell bent on getting even, be warned that it can be a very costly business indeed. The newspapers love to report the stories about what couples can do to each other but they rarely tell you that these destructive actions can cost you dear when it comes to negotiating your settlement.

Revenge is a way of hitting back if one party feels they've been poorly served by the other. For example:

- the reason for the divorce as cited on the petition
- an adulterous affair,
- parsimony/greed when it comes to the finances
- the arrangements for the children.

While women appear to be much more materially minded and security-conscious *during* a relationship, they can show scant respect or a man's treasured possessions when it comes to divorce. Credit card debts have been run up to the maximum. Irreplaceable objects such as expensive cars, vintage wine and valuable sporting equipment have been destroyed by vengeful partners. All of which, in high a proportion of cases, have resulted in the perpetrator's financial settlement being drastically reduced to cover the cost. In fact, the cost of the damage is deducted from any settlement, or taken into account during the proceedings.

It is also generally a frame of mind that attacks during the seven stages of divorce listed in Chapter One, especially when there's a lull in the proceedings or you've just heard from your solicitor that your ex- isn't going to meet your demands. Anyone who has been through the divorce process will probably confess to one or all of the following:

Breakdown
Unless you've given your partner just cause' for divorce (i.e. sexual misdemeanour or violence) it may come as a bit of a surprise to read via the divorce petition what a bitch/bastard you've been. If you feel the accusations are unjust and untrue, then it would be understandable in anyone's book should you wish to retaliate. Just

remember that in the present legal climate, someone has got to be the guilty party' and that your partner's solicitor has got to make sure your 'unreasonable behaviour' is convincing enough for a divorce to be granted. Resist the urge to start trading insults or stretching cling-film across the toilet bowl!

Shock
When people go into shock, they go numb — which means they prefer to play the guilt card by using the children as canon fodder, or revenge by proxy. Don't leave a well-thumbed edition of *Anna Karenina* next to the razor, or sleeping pills in the bathroom

Anger
Plain, good old-fashioned anger will purge the humiliation you feel about being dumped, or turned out of your own home. Make a mental note that if anything gets damaged it's going to come out of *your* share of the settlement, so go for minimum liability, maximum effect. Resist the urge to trash the car or wardrobe, and concentrate your efforts on creating some social discomfort via a mutual gossip.

Pain
If there's anyone else in the frame then there's sport to be had at their expense. After all, the new lover will shortly be taking your place, so rediscover the foulest aspect of your soon-to-be-ex's personal habits and have evidence of them delivered to the love-nest. A rather unsavoury collection of well-thumbed and explicit porn mags has been used in the past.

Hatred
This is a rather dangerous stage of the proceedings where things can go pear-shaped if you're not careful. There's nothing stopping you from wishing your ex at the Second Circle of Hell along with all the other fornicating, lying bastards/bitches but you've got to find a way of getting them there without it (a) costing you money, (b) having a court injunction slapped on you, or (c) standing trial for murder.

Grief

Take a leaf straight out of *Dido and Aeneas* and go for noble suffering. The blazing funeral pyre might be taking things a bit too far, but there's still plenty of mileage to be gained from being seen to be rising resplendent from your own ashes.

Acceptance

Okay so you might have forgiven but you sure as hell ain't going to forgive. Go for a change of image, get yourself a life and leave your ex- worrying about why you never looked that way for him/her.

Never lose sight of the fact that extracting revenge may backfire if taken to extremes. At best you can claim temporary insanity but as Midge found out to her cost, small towns have long memories and every chap she when out with following her divorce, soon got to hear about the way she'd driven Ted's BMW to the local quarry and tipped it over the edge. This kind of behaviour convinces people that not only have you completely lost the plot, but that you might do something similar to them if they cause you any upset.

You may think you're in control but in reality, it's the reverse

PICKING UP THE PIECES

Starting over again following the break-up of a violent relationship is not easy for the simple reason that it is much more difficult to put our faith and trust in another man or woman.

 Lucy remarried but she let it be known in no uncertain terms that if her new husband so much as raised his hand to her, she would be off; they have now been married for over twenty years.

A leading psychiatrist maintains that we can recognise certain behaviour patterns or disordered personalities, in those more prone to aggression or violence. According to Dr Raj Persaud, there are three types of disordered personality:

⇒ those who prefer fantasy to reality
⇒ novelty or thrill seekers
⇒ those who are over-cautious and/or pessimistic

Couple any of the above with an immature personality and you have someone who may be prone to withdrawal or aggressive behaviour. "These indicate an inability to control impulses, which thus produces behaviour problems, like temper tantrums, or hitting someone when angry, or refusing to come out of your room to talk to your family when upset," writes Dr Persaud. "The problem for these people is that their relationships are always torrid: one moment they have met Mr Perfect, but when he blots his copybook, the next day they think they are going out with the most awful man in the world."

Recognising the warning signs

Current research in America has also shown that men with a higher level of testosterone are less likely to marry and those who do marry are more likely to get divorced. This link between high testosterone levels, dominance and competition suggests that such men tend to carry 'contentious competitive behaviour' into their relationship with the opposite sex. The result may be that they are unable to sustain a relationship and divorce, or they may have a poor quality marriage. Aggressive and dominating behaviour may be fine in the boardroom, or on the sports field, but it is hardly conducive to a happy marriage.

Although the levels of testosterone in men are between twenty to forty times higher than those in women, recent studies have confirmed that the levels increase quite considerably in women in positions of power. and are much higher in aggressive women. If we return to the observations of divorce lawyer Vanessa Lloyd Platt, we find evidence that a growing number of men are complaining about this female aggression that is manifesting more and more in divorce cases.

Picking up the pieces means learning to recognise the warning signs and steering clear of anyone who exhibits any of the above traits. A violent relationship leaves its scars and the last thing anyone wants is to find themselves in a similar situation again.

VIEWPOINTS FROM THE LAYMAN'S ARMS

When the Meg Mathews-Noel Gallagher marriage ended, the media reported that she would be seeking a £10 million divorce settlement despite the fact that the couple had reportedly made a pre-nuptial agreement that gave Ms Mathews £100,000 if the marriage broke up. According to the press, she had been offered £3 million but instead wanted £7 million in cash, plus a £1.5 million holiday home in Ibiza and a £1.5 million London flat. If couples make a pre-nuptial agreement, shouldn't they be bound by law to keep it?

Male response:
"Sorry, Meg Mathews should take the original agreement and shut up. It is *his* money; he earned it all. This is nothing less than sheer greed on her part."

"This is obviously a new career move for scheming women. Find a wealthy sucker, find a way of getting him to marry you and then go for a divorce and half his assets. With the law going the way it is, no man in his right mind would ever consider getting married."

Female response:
"Yes — an agreement is an agreement. Hard luck, Meg. Take the settlement and shut up. He earned it — she is a freeloader.'

"I think the law should take into account why a couple are getting divorced in circumstances like this, and particularly where there are no children involved. He's the one with the earning potential, she could never make that sort of money on her own."

Chapter Seven

Setting Up A New Home

In the event of a divorce, one partner at least has to find alternative accommodation. More often than not, it's the absent parent who is forced to walk away with no capital, since this is tied up in the marital home until the children finish their education. If the matrimonial home is sold and the profits shared then both parties will be looking for somewhere affordable to live. Whatever you do, it will be necessary to provide yourself with a roof and this can be an extremely daunting task, especially for those who find themselves divorced when they are getting near to retirement age.

Moving home at any time is an accepted 'highly stressful life event'. For the divorcee the stress is compounded by the additional upheaval of packing your belongings, discarding and leaving behind what is, in effect, a very large part of your life. Financial considerations will probably mean the necessity of looking for a smaller house or flat that will be suitable for your personal needs.

BUYING OR RENTING?

A high percentage of divorced people feel that the only route open to them is to rent accommodation since they have little, if any, capital to put down as a deposit on a new home.

Buying:

These days it is possible to obtain a 100% mortgage that will allow you to borrow the full purchase price. All you need to find is the stamp duty, valuation and legal fees, and any other costs associated with buying a house. Some 100% mortgages will even cover these additional costs as part of the loan. Many 100% mortgages come with a Mortgage Indemnity Guarantee Premium that can run into thousands of pounds but it is possible to avoid it if you know where to look.

Bear in mind that as with any type of loan, 100% mortgages are not without risk and it might be worth consulting an independent mortgage adviser who:

⇒ knows which are the best deals;
⇒ makes sure that any penalties for paying of the loan earlier are not extortionate;
⇒ ensures there are no restrictive clauses and that the fees charged are not excessive.

There are one or two other points to consider if you and your ex- agree that one should buy the other out.

1. The buyer may have to pay additional stamp duty on his or her ex-partner's half of the mortgage. Stamp duty can be avoided if the transfer of the property is made as a result of a court order arising out of divorce proceedings, but you should consult a solicitor.

2. Do not make any *private* arrangements should you and your ex- agree that one of you should take over the mortgage. Unless a transfer is registered with the building society, who will then formally release one partner from the mortgage (providing they are satisfied the payments will be met), the property will still legally belong to both of you and the outgoing partner may be entitled to make a claim against the equity several years down the line.

Pluses:
Even if you've only managed to buy a small house or flat, you've got your feet back on the property ladder.

Minuses:
If you've obtained a Court Order for maintenance, under the new CSA laws it will not take your new mortgage into account if your ex- decides to have the maintenance agreement amended to obtain more money.

Renting:

It's easier to rent in some parts of the country than others; in some areas it can be a much more expensive option. Property is usually let on a six month (with option of renewal) lease and under normal circumstances you will be required to pay the first month's rent, together with a deposit that the landlord can off-set against any repairs or redecorating that may be necessary when you leave the property. Make sure you know exactly what your liability will be before signing the tenancy agreement. Renting may be the only option if you are unable to obtain a mortgage either because of financial restrictions or age.

Pluses:

Renting means that you have a place to live short-term while you sort out your options. If gives you the time to take stock of your financial position and plan for the future without the permanency of a mortgage commitment.

Minuses:

Since tenancy agreements are usually for a six month period and a landlord can get you out within 28 days, there is very little security in rented accommodation.

Considering other options

Other options for finding a home might be tempting in the short-term but it's easy to stub your toe on contracts and clauses if you're not thinking clearly because of the divorce. Buying a property with a friend (and fellow-divorcee) may seem like an ideal solution but what happens if your 'tenant-in-common' decides to move out or remarry? One can buy the other's share of the property but there may be all sorts of financial and legal implications, especially if you each put down different sized deposits, or pay a different portion of the mortgage. It is also important to ensure that it would be possible to buy each other out in the long-term; check with the bank or building society *before* signing anything.

Also bear in mind that this arrangement places your future credit rating in the hands of another. If anything goes wrong and they can't afford to pay their share of the mortgage, *you* can become a 'bad debt' even though you continue to pay your portion and the property will be re-possessed by the bank or building society. Also accept that you could both cause the other a lot of problems if you don't take out accident, sickness and unemployment (ASU) cover which ensures that the mortgage is paid if either of you are unable to work. Be warned, however, premiums are high and it is important to read the small print carefully. Equally important is the need to take out life assurance that will pay out a lump sum if one of you dies.

Should you decide to go ahead, it may be worth considering drawing up a legal agreement through a solicitor setting out exactly who is entitled to what in the event of one of you moving out at a later date.

Anticipating problems

Renting a property with a friend or fellow-divorcee can also present problems if both names aren't included on the tenancy agreement. Should one decide to move out, you could find yourself homeless if you're not named as a joint tenant on the lease, because there is no automatic right to occupy the property, even if you've lived there right from the start. Property agents acting on behalf of a landlord manage a large proportion of rental accommodation, so they tend to stick to the letter of the law rather than compromise their client's business interests. If you are unsure about the agreement, take it to the Citizen's Advice Bureau or a solicitor before signing.

Very often, divorced people find themselves in the position of having to take a job doing the only thing they know how to do: live-in housekeeping or gardening. This accommodation, of course, goes with the job and if for any reason you are unable to continue to work, you will have to leave.

PUTTING DISTANCE BETWEEN YOU

Whatever the circumstances behind the divorce, this may be the time to consider making other changes for your future — by changing from country to town living, or vice versa. Take into account the differences in the cost of living between one part of the country and another but do be realistic about what you want and what you can cater for. The rural idyll might be everyone's dream but the reality is often of short duration; conversely you might wish to return to your 'roots' and exchange the faster pace of urban living for something more peaceful.

If you plan to move from one end of the country to another, do make sure (as far as you can) that you will be able to settle. The reality of the North-South divide, for example, is less to do with money and more concerned with outlook.

Nell has just settled down after a ten-year move around the country following a break-up of a long-term relationship. "I'm Home Counties by birth and after a stint in London decided to move to rural Wales with my new partner for a fresh start. Although we were miles from Swansea or Cardiff, the local social life couldn't be bettered. The local community theatre put on everything from fringe cinema, classical music, popular and classic productions to folk music and pantomime - there's was something for everyone. Our Welsh neighbours were some of the most hospitable folk I've ever met and we were always included in any invitations from the village.

"Following the break-up I had to go for an affordable property and, having moved to the Midlands, haven't been anywhere in two years. Although I have an eclectic taste in entertainment, the local theatre hasn't put on one thing that I'd want to sit through. Although I live on a small estate, I haven't yet had an invite to call in to a neighbour's house for coffee despite my own invitations. People are polite enough but apparently, they think I'm 'posh'. I'm shortly moving fifty miles away into the next county where I've found the people friendlier and the local entertainment much more to my taste. It's amazing what a different those few miles have made."

Whatever your decision, it's not easy to house hunt from a distance unless you know the area exceptionally well. It can be quite a drain on your finances if you're travelling back and forth to look at houses if you don't have friends or family with whom you can visit. It is, however, in your best interest to stay for a few days in the area in order to assess the locality but don't be tempted to move because a friend lives nearby. If the friendship doesn't come up to expectation you could land up feeling even more isolated than ever.

THE OLDER YOU GET ...

... the more you'll need to consider local facilities in terms of social facilities, shops, chemist, healthcare and public transport if your settlement does not include a car. The older we get the more discerning we become and unless we've really primed ourselves with the fact that the new property *isn't* going to be as large or luxurious as the marital home, it's going to be an uphill struggle finding somewhere suitable.

Make a check-list of all the essential features your new home must have, i.e. number of rooms, location, local facilities, garden, etc., and any aspects that are non-negotiable. For example, one divorcee refused to even consider any property with a downstairs bathroom. "I'd grown up in a cottage with a downstairs bathroom and it was an absolute nightmare," said Sue. "People thought I was mad because I wouldn't even look at a house with a downstairs extension but since I knew I wouldn't be buying it, I'd just be wasting everyone's time."

Have several photocopies made and take a fresh one with you each time you view a property; make any necessary notes to provide a reminder of what took your fancy. It is important to try to visualise what the place will look like with your furniture in place, and if you have any large items to consider, make sure you've got a tape-measure to check on the size of the rooms. It's also a good idea to take a small compass and check the alignment of the house so that you can tell which rooms benefit from maximum sunshine and which way the garden faces.

Making sure it's what you want

Just remember that no house will meet your exact requirements, so take the following into consideration:

- ✓ is the flat/house what you want?
- ✓ does the layout suit your requirements?
- ✓ is there enough room?
- ✓ will your existing equipment/furniture fit?
- ✓ is the location right for you?
- ✓ is the property in good repair?
- ✓ will you be able to maintain/decorate the property yourself?
- ✓ will you be able to manage the garden without help?
- ✓ can you take the family pets?

We don't like to think we're getting older but if we're looking at buying a property once we've reached our fifties, we need to make sure there are adequate facilities should failing health mean we can't negotiate the stairs in ten year's time. Huge gardens may give a great deal of pleasure now, but will they become an insurmountable problem in later years?

MOVING ON UP, MOVING ON OUT

Moving house is a traumatic time under normal circumstances but having to pack up your own personal belongings to move out of the family home will magnify the upset a hundred fold. Regardless of whether you have divided your assets 50/50, or whether all you have is a van-load of personal items, take the trouble to pack everything properly.

Allow as much time as possible to sort out what you will be taking and for the packing. Sort any unwanted possessions into saleable items and what could go to the local charity shop. Under the circumstances, disposing of personal things can be difficult but were talking about a fresh start and so be ruthless about getting rid of items that have outlived their usefulness – you will not do it once you have moved and it will just find its way into the back of another cupboard.

If you are taking ornaments, china and glass remember that it isn't the newspaper that protects them so much as the resilience of *crumpled* paper. Put a thick layer at the bottom of the tea-chest or box and do not put the heavier items on top of smaller, more fragile ones. Mark the boxes 'fragile' and identify the contents because you will *not* remember which is which — trust me! Put sticky coloured labels on the *side* of each container so that they show up if the boxes are stacked on top of each other.

Personal items that may need special packing or will be difficult to move:

- original pictures/limited edition prints
- stereo system and CD collection
- specialist collections
- antique furniture and/or ornaments
- books (any large number)
- computer equipment
- wine
- valuables (lodge with your bank)

During the upset of divorce you may be tempted to just fling everything into a box and store it in a friend's garage but in time to come, you'll regret it. Items such as family photographs with all their attendant memories (such as the wedding album) could be lodged with either of the grandparents, so that the children can have them at a later date. Photographs are a reminder of better days and if there is a temptation to destroy them, remember that in later years you will be depriving your children of their own family history. If you do not have children's feelings to consider - burn 'em!

CHANGING ADDRESS

You may not want to go into a long and involved explanation with everyone on your Christmas card list about your break-up and the easiest way to get around the problem is to use your personal computer to produce something that is self-explanatory. Phillip used this device to inform friends and family that:

> *"Phillip and Charley, the dog, are moving to*
> *(new address) ... (phone number)*
> *Carol and the kids are remaining at*
> *(old address) ... (phone number)*
> *Any letters and 'phone calls will be appreciated*
> *once we 're settled in after ... (date)"*

The choice of whether they wish to keep in touch or not, is back in their court and it saves the embarrassment of people having to ask either of you for the other's forwarding address.

A formal notification of your move should be sent to:

☑ Finances: Even if you do not intend to move your account, you will need to notify the bank of your new address. This also applies to all savings accounts, building societies, Premium Bonds and National Savings.

☑ Pension/Benefits: Notify your local social security office and give the address of the new post office/bank account. If your pension is paid quarterly notify the DSS Central Pensions Branch.

☑ National Insurance: Notify the social security office of the old and new address, giving your National Insurance number.

☑ Inland Revenue: Inform your Inspector of Taxes

☑ Stocks/Shares: write to the registrar and inform your financial advisor.

☑ Credit Cards: All accounts which are paid weekly or monthly by post will need to be notified, and any local charge accounts closed if you are moving out of the area.

☑ Television rental: Check with the hire firm to see whether you can transfer the existing agreement to your new address or whether you will be required to surrender the equipment.

☑ Mail Order: Selected mail order catalogues can be re-directed by sending details of your change of address and quoting your personal reference number.

☑ Car: You will need to amend the details of your vehicle registration, driving licence, motor insurance and the relevant motoring organisation.

☑ Insurance: Personal insurers will need to be notified, together with any amendments to your contents/house insurance.

☑ NHS: Inform doctors, dentists, hospitals, clinics or day centres; National Blood Transfusion Service.

☑ Societies/Professional organisations: Will need change of address details tm update their records.

☑ Memberships/Clubs: Including book, wine and sports clubs.

☑ Library: Cancel ticket and return all books

☑ Theatre, concert or other mailing lists: Amend their records or cancel if you are moving out of the area.

☑ Mail order firms: Request a redirection of catalogues, etc.,

Despite advising everyone about your change of address, there are always a few that slip through the net. The Post Office will redirect your mail for a period of one month, three months or a year on receipt of an official form and the appropriate fee. This form also has a section for notifying the National TV Licence Records Office of your change of address. In the case of divorce it is advisable to have mail re-directed by the Post Office just in case your ex-harbours any incendiary intentions towards your mail.

FINANCIAL RESPONSIBILITIES

Concerns about rising levels of personal debt have led the Government to form a 'task force' to examine whether ease of access to credit and lack of controls are leading more people into debt. Since 1997, when the average personal debt placed with a debt management company was £10,000, the figures have almost *trebled* by 2004. Other alarming shifts show that debt has spread from low income groups to so-called middle-England and that while four years ago the majority of debtors were in their late twenties, they are more likely to be in their mid-thirties.

For the newly divorced, the need to re-finance their lives can lead to an over-indulgence on the 'plastic'. Having been used to a comfortably furnished home and a reasonable life-style, it's extremely difficult to suddenly cut back on our expenditure. The problem is, that we no longer have the income to pay the bills and often find we can only manage to meet the monthly 'minimum payment'. We've all been there and worn that particular t.-shirt.

Finding help with debt

If you find yourself in debt, free help and advice services are provided by the Citizen's Advice Bureaux and organisations such as the Consumer Credit Counselling Service who will spend time to familiarise themselves with the problem and advise on what to do to pay creditors, how to keep the roof over your head, and ensure continuing services such as gas and electricity. The advice and help given is tailored to the individual and continues until you are out of trouble.

Taking out life assurance

Another area which is causing concern is the fact that nearly one in three parents has no life assurance, which means that their dependants might find themselves homeless should the family earner die unexpectedly. The main reason for this situation is that many mortgage lenders no longer make life assurance a condition of the loan, while a growing number of homebuyers take the opportunity to cut costs when applying for a mortgage. Although mortgage holders seem willing to cover themselves against illness or accident preventing them from working, fewer seem to look at the worse case scenario.

Even if you are not looking at buying another home, it is still advisable to take out some form of life assurance if you have dependants who are likely to suffer financial hardship in the advent of your untimely death. There are low cost schemes available that will cover the cost of the mortgage but if you intend to provide sufficient capital to maintain a reasonable standard of living then you would be well advised to consult a life insurance broker.

Before discussing the options, work out how much you spend on household bills (including the mortgage), food, clothes, car and other expenses during the course of a year. Armed with this information you can then investigate all the alternative schemes available before choosing. Do bear in mind, however, that although the monthly payments vary widely. a lot will depend on your age and that a 50-year old can pay three times the amount per month of a 30-year old because of the shorter term the cover has to run.

FURNISHING ON A TIGHT BUDGET

Everything runs up bills with a new home and most of us can't resist the urge to run up huge credit card debts when buying new furnishings. If you've been forced out of the family home without the benefit of sharing the contents, then you're faced with no option other than to replace, which will probably take a good-sized bite out of your income. In all honesty, an absent father paying maintenance for his children won't have much left over for the luxuries of expensive furnishings.

If you've been used to shopping at the best stores in town, you may have to get used to cutting according to your cloth and shop around. There are discount warehouses in every small town and this doesn't necessarily mean poor quality. Carpets, furnishings and bedding can be picked up at a reasonable cost if you're willing to put in the effort to discover where you can get the best deal. Bargains can still be found in second-hand furniture shops.

Carol picked up some of her best bits of furniture by scouring the local junk shops. "It's amazing what you can find when you go out to look. My computer system sits on an old pot board that has polished up beautifully. People might turn their nose up at the thought of looking in junk shops for furniture but it's a hundred times better than those awful flimsy work-stations I see in all my more affluent friend's homes these days"

Listing your needs

Once the divorce has got to settlement stage, you should make a list of *everything* you are going to need in order of priority. For a childless couple it should be reasonably easy to divide the house contents (see Chapter Three) but where one partner is being forced to leave the house and contents for the benefit of the children, the guidelines are less flexible. When it comes down to agreeing terms via your solicitor, don't be slow in requesting the furnishings from the guest bedroom, for example, or the family's third television set. Divide your list into categories such as:

Essential items:

Kitchen equipment (cooker, fridge/freezer, washing machine, cooking utensils. saucepans, kettle and iron); bed and bedding; towels; curtains; china and cutlery; glasses; comfortable chairs; etc.,

Non-essential items:

Carpets; dining table and chairs; bedroom furniture; sofa; storage units; light fittings; dishwasher; etc.,

Luxuries:
Lamps; pictures; plants; mirrors; rugs; book shelves; occasional tables; etc.,

Obviously everyone's list of essential and non-essential items will differ according to their taste and life-style; some would class a dishwasher as a luxury, rather than a non-essential item. Many, however, would put it at the top of their list of essential items, together with a tumble-dryer. A list of whatever you feel to be *your* priorities will help to budget when it comes to furnishing your new home.

Because she was moving into a much smaller home, Pamela needed to replace all her kitchen appliances and soon found there was an additional expense. "Everything electrical comes with maintenance offer these days and if I'd taken up the option on every single item, I'd have been paying out well over £100 per month on the instalments. At that rate I figured if something went wrong after the guarantee ran out, it would be cheaper to buy a replacement rather than spend £1000+ a year 'just in case'. And to be honest, I couldn't afford it."

If you've always left this kind of shopping to your husband or wife, it can come as quite a shock to discover just how much things cost these days. This is where you need to keep a firm control over the urge to ignore the fact that you can't afford it but spend anyway. If you've come this far and got through the divorce proceedings relatively unscathed, it's only the next step to assume full financial control over your life

MANAGING ON A REDUCED INCOME

It's not always easy to economise, even for the rich and famous. One poor soul had to give up her private jet because her £9 million settlement wouldn't cover the cost. "This will mean a major cut in her life-style," said her solicitor at the time. Although the divorce laws have undergone some radical changes in the past year following the Law Lords decree that the courts should now no longer discriminate between husband and wife and their respective roles. ("There should be no bias in favour of the money-earner and against the home-maker and the child-carer.") The 50/50 split hinted at by Lord Nicholls does not necessarily mean that a presumption of equal division could be read into the law.

The two cases that changed the course of financial settlement (*Cowan v. Cowan* and *White v. White*) still leave lawyers in a quandary over advising their clients exactly what constitutes a fair or equal settlement; does it means half of everything, or just the assets acquired during the marriage? Whatever the ruling, it still means that divorce will effectively halve your *spendable* income whether you're a Stock Market trader or a market stall trader. The court will agree a figure to be paid each week/month and you will either have to manage on what you get - or whatever you're left with once the maintenance payments have been taken out.

For ordinary people like us, having to manage on a reduced income can be the final straw that leads to severe depression and/or debt. Once we've taken the 'essentials' out (i.e. council tax, rent, heating and lighting) there may not be much left over no matter how often you rework the sums.

"My downfall came as a result of the direct debits," said Cindy. "All my major out-goings were paid this way and at the end of the day there was very little left for food. As a result I was constantly overdrawn at the bank. Then the bank stopped some of my cheques and the bank charges began to mount up. I was in a no-win situation until I got in touch with the Consumer Credit Counselling Service. They advised on how to keep manage my income and expenditure and still pay off my debts."

It must be obvious by now that the greatest long-term problem caused by divorce is money, or the question of the division of it, when a couple splits up. Ironically, even the new legislation is geared up to handle the money-question, not the pressing necessity of allowing couples to make life less stressful by being able to obtain a 'no fault' divorce. Changes within the CSA means that it is no longer possible to make a mutually acceptable settlement and call it quits. The new ruling means that the parent with care can keep pushing for more and more money from the absent parent when in many cases, malice will probably be the governing motive rather than need.

Keeping control

The lack of finances can be a major cause of depression among divorcees and often the cause for people taking their own lives, especially if they are hounded by agencies such as the CSA, or they feel they have not been treated fairly by the court. Depression often follows what are termed as 'exit events' such as divorce or the break-up of a long-term relationship; and after divorce men appear to suffer more from mental health problems than women.

The lack of finances may also prevent the absent parent from seeing their children should their ex- have moved out of the area. If the loss of family and home can trigger depression, then an additional financial burden resulting from a divorce they didn't instigate, has pushed a large number of men to commit suicide.

Keeping control under these circumstances is extremely difficult and unless you have friends who can offer constructive, practical help, you may be better off seeking professional help before the situation gets completely out of control.

TELEPHONE LIFE-LINE

For most of us picking up the pieces after a divorce, the telephone becomes an essential lifeline and so do be prepared for a nasty shock when the bill comes in! Often the only way to defeat the loneliness of sitting alone every evening is to dial a friend's number and the next thing you know, an hour has gone by at peak call time.

Do spare a thought for those on the receiving end of your mind-numbing conversations, and listen for the warning signs that they are becoming bored with the subject. Do they:

- lapse into long silences while you talk

- make periodic non-committal grunting noises

- keep trying to change the subject

- cut the conversation short

- frequently make excuses to get off the phone

- get a family member to say they're not in

- start leaving the ansaphone on

- fail to return your calls

The above are fair indications that you've run out of sympathy time and that you'd better get a grip on life before your best friends disappear altogether. No-one minds lending a sympathetic ear but divorces tend to drag on for quite a long time and we can't expect our friends to sit and listen to an extended, weekly blow-by-blow account of the proceedings. If you fancy a chat make sure you've got some *positive* news to impart and try to keep it brief until the old rapport returns.

Handy tips:

- Set the cookery timer for 15 minutes and cut the conversation when your time's up.

- Have a telephone box and 'pay' every time you use the 'phone or buy stamps each week from the Post Office.

- Keep the mobile for emergencies or have a look at the many options that might be better value when you have to watch your budget, like pay-as-you-go instead of a monthly bill.

- Try to make your calls in the evenings or at weekends at the cheaper rate

- Check with British Telecom or your present telephone company about their best tariffs for 'friends and family'.

The telephone *is* a life-time in times of trouble but we need to keep a tight control on our emotions if we're going to use as an instrument of pleasurable communication and not as a life-raft.

A MATTER OF WILL POWER

Although we mentioned making a new will in the 'legal bit', this is a good time to re-evaluate your assets, and what you what to happen to them should you meet an untimely death. Sorting things out now can prevent any distressing disputes over who is entitled to your property when you die. Although making a will is something we find a chore, it is nothing to the upset and aggravation for families of someone who dies intestate.

Points to ponder:

- The laws governing intestacy do not allow the estate to pass automatically to his or her spouse.

- If you are co-habiting, your partner could receive nothing.

- If you do not leave a will the Government decides who benefits and it may not necessarily pass to the people you think it will.

- If you are married and die intestate, your spouse is only entitled to the first £200,000 of your estate with a life interest in the remainder. The balance goes to your next of kin, be it parents, siblings or long-lost distant relatives.

- If you are married with children, your spouse is entitled to £125,000 of your estate with a life interest in half of the rest. The other half passes to your children when they reach the age of 18.

- If you wish step-children (or friends) to benefit, you must make a will.

- Unmarried partners with no wills only begin to have an interest in each other's estate after two years of cohabiting.

You may feel that you're too young to make a will, or at this particular point in time you have nothing worthwhile to leave, or that it's just something else to think about at a time when you can do without the hassle. Even if it's only ensuring that your best friend gets to sort out your personal effects, it's worth taking the time. You can appoint anyone you like to execute your will, including beneficiaries but if you appoint a solicitor, accountant or banker, they will probably charge a fee.

There are three main ways of making a will:

i.   The safest way if there is an amount of money and/or property involved is through a solicitor and you can expect to pay around £90.

ii.   You could use the will-making service provided by a bank for around £65

iii.   If your assets are limited you can draw up your own will using a will form available from most stationers, bearing in mind that if you get it wrong, it could become invalid.

Wills are a way of making sure that the people you want to benefit get what you want them to have. This is all about keeping control of your affairs.

VIEWPOINTS FROM THE LAYMAN'S ARMS

Kate is currently taking her medical degree. Andrew has paid for her to go through medical school and taken care of their four-year old daughter while his wife completed her studies. Kate plans to go into the better-paying private sector once she's qualified and has decided that she now wants a divorce. She was expecting Andrew to continue to support both her and the child, and is surprised that he has refused, saying that he will also apply to be awarded 'parent with care'. Kate is miffed but can she really expect any more financial support from Andrew?

Male response:
"No way! She seems to have a totally selfish attitude to life and needs to leave the man alone."

"No. He has done all he can to support the family unit and should expect her to support them from her future earnings."

Female response:
"I don't think she should have anymore financial support. Andrew has provided for and supported her throughout her studies and, in the private sector, she will probably earn more than him anyway. Is she going to pay back the money she's cost him over the years?"

"Kate is being totally unreasonable. She expects too much. It is clear that she is well able to support herself so why should Andrew be expected to supplement her prospective income? He has more than fulfilled any obligations as a husband."

Chapter Eight

Setting Yourself A Goal

This is the time for change but no one can bring about *positive* change but yourself. There's an old adage in transpersonal circles that you cannot change anything but yourself but, in changing yourself, you will find that the world changes around you. There is little point, for example, in harbouring the ambition to become a best-selling novelist if you've never written a word of fiction in your life. Joining a local writers' circle could be the first step but only you can make that positive move towards changing your circumstances.

There's no point in wishing, praying and hoping that something profound will happen to alter your way of life without making some effort. Otherwise you become like the chap who prayed incessantly to win the Lottery. The prayers became more fervent and demanding as the weeks, months and years went by until God finally sent down a message: "Okay, okay, but at least meet me halfway and buy a ticket!"

GETTING RID OF UNWANTED BAGGAGE
The methods of getting rid of unwanted baggage will largely depend on whether you are a team-player or a solitary creature. Here we are talking about all those unnecessary things that keep us locked into the past, that we don't really need but from which we're afraid to cut ourselves loose. The past, they say, is another country and it's time to jettison all those useless emotions and belongings that will prevent us from moving forward.

Divorce Recovery Workshop
The first Divorce Recovery Workshop was based on a concept brought back from America in 1992. The idea had been offered to various care groups but a lack of response prompted the decision to finance and run a workshop independently. Thirty people

attended and completed the course but their enthusiasm for the material was overwhelming. On completion they formed their own social support group and on one of their rambles requested another workshop.

It was quickly realised, however, that despite its success, isolated workshops could never meet the national need. It was also clear that the way forward for the Divorce Recovery Workshop movement was for it to be run as a self-help group by people who had been through it themselves. To facilitate this, the course was documented with the material redesigned to make it easy for those with basic organisation and group dynamic skills to promote and run an effective self-resourcing programme of workshops.

The second workshop was used to test this documented approach. Fifty-five people — both men and women - completed the course with the same positive response to the material. Apart from using the original co-ordinator, the entire event was run by participants from the first workshop. The format was further tested with the third workshop and this time the workshop was run entirely by a co-ordinator and facilitators selected from previous workshops. The results were so encouraging that workshops in the Thames Valley area have run twice each year since with attendances of between 30 to 60 people each time and have contributed substantially to financing the National programme.

The founders of the DRW were quick to realise that the depth of emotional suffering of the newly separated or divorced was not generally realised. While society allows the bereaved years to adjust, the divorced are frequently expected to 'pull them selves together' in a matter of weeks, unaided.

The DRW offers:

- a service that is suitable for anyone, male and female, of any age, at any stage of separation or divorce.

- a six-week course of evening sessions that helps the individual come to terms with a relationship that has irretrievably broken down.

- a better understanding of what each individual is going through, provides them with support from others in the same situation, and assists in the process of re-adjustment in their lives.

- a secure environment for discussion and understanding of feelings. It also provides a new circle of friends when the workshop is over.

- a nationwide self-help group run by volunteers who have attended the workshop – there are no 'experts' but all those present will have personally experienced a relationship break up.

Tricia Lockhart, who handles the original publicity for the Divorce Recovery Workshop said that although men appeared to be more reluctant to approach the organisation in the beginning, 25% of the participants were male. "Once they've completed the course, a larger proportion of men are more willing to stay on as volunteers to help others through the recovery process," she added.

GETTING ON WITH THE JOB

For many, however, this approach would be their idea of Purgatory, since they don't relate to any form of group participation on emotional issues. The concept of unburdening themselves in public would produce the same reaction as suggesting that they undress in the street. Here we are talking about the private people who epitomise the 'stiff upper-lip' brigade and who still firmly believe that personal problems should not be subjected to public scrutiny.

For Justine it would go against everything she'd been brought up to believe in. "To me, this is outside interference and would only bring about the deepest resentment."

From David, a retired military man, the reaction was the same. "Definitely *not* for me. I'd be a pretty poor sort of a chap if I couldn't out my own affairs without having to turn to a complete stranger."

In the present climate of counselling and group therapy, those who decline to participate are often accused of being mentally or emotionally insecure. Their 'failure' to interact with a group of people in similar circumstances is seen as being some sort of rejection of the new caring/sharing social order. This way of thinking isn't a 'class thing' since it has its adherents from all walks of life and backgrounds. Families who grew up being intensely private (for whatever reason) prefer to sort out their own domestic upheavals — and are pretty good at doing so.

Deciding what support you need

Like all things in life, the choice of whether you feel the need for support from those in similar circumstances, or keep your own counsel, should be your *own* decision. The fact that you come from a family background that frowns upon organisations such as the Divorce Recovery Workshop should not prevent you from joining a group if *you* think it will help. Particularly if, like many men, there is no one in whom you feel you can confide when things start to get rough.

To help you decide, try asking yourself the following:

- Has your divorce left you feeling isolated?

- Has the divorce cut you off from friends

- Do you have close friends/family in whom you can confide?

- Can they offer sensible, practical advice or help?

- Does your upbringing discourage seeking outside help?

- Would talking to a counsellor put things in perspective?

- Do you believe that you can cope on your own?

- Do you need help?

An honest appraisal of your answers should indicate whether to explore the possibilities of joining a local or national group. Remember, however, the whole aim is to act as a support while you help yourself — the group is not there to sort out your problems. Here you will find practical advice and people who are going through the same difficulties and who are, therefore, more willing to listen.

A CHANGE OF IMAGE

Known in the legal profession as the 'break-over' this phenomena is the change of appearance that occurs as a direct result of a broken relationship. When Vanessa Feltz's husband announced that one of the reasons he'd been attracted to someone else was because she was too fat, she dieted, hired a personal trainer and lost five stone. Julia Carling sported the 'girl next door' image until her divorce from rugby-playing Will turned her into a glamorous television presenter. When Anthea Turner pinched Della Bovey's husband, Grant, Della's transformation from frumpy mum to stylish lady was so startling that he returned home — albeit temporarily.

This is an area on which we should all focus our attention, regardless of the position we find ourselves in — and whether male or female. Appearance counts for a lot when it comes to splitting up. It may not in itself be one of the compound issues listed in Chapter One but an ex-partner's appearance *will* creep into the equation sooner or later.

Some men cite the fact that their wife is being to look and sound like her mother; or that she no longer bothers to shave under her armpits and it only seen wearing jogging pants and a sweatshirt. Women may no longer want sex with an animated barrel of lard but equally they can well live without a middle-aged husband trying to squeeze himself into 28-inch waist jeans in a desperate attempt to still appear 'trendy'.

Both will read this type of behaviour as being outward signs that the other no longer cares about them or what they think.

When Carolyn suggested that Stuart stopped wearing his collection of ear-studs, he took this as a sign that she no longer found him attractive and promptly started an affair with a girl 10 years his junior.

Take the cross-gender mirror-test and be honest. Whether your male or female, take all your clothes off and stand in front of a full-length mirror.

Are you over-weight?
We all put on a little bit of weight as we get older and our metabolism changes and if you're ultra-thin, this can be to your advantage from the long-term health point of view, if, on the other hand, there's a mass of flab and a sagging stomach ask yourself whether you'd fancy yourself if you were a wo/man? Have you expected your partner to put up with this rather unpleasant sight? Make no bones about it *both men and women* find obesity offensive if it's a result of over-indulgence and a lack of self-control when it comes to dietary habits. On top of that, it's down right unhealthy for you, too!

Does your hair-style need attention?
A change of hair-style can do wonders for low self-esteem and can, in some circumstances, alter the whole way you feel about yourself and life in general. Women, in particular recognise the important of the drastic new hair cut when life is at a low point — so go mad and do something about it. The long hair *v.* 40-plus arguments always cite celebrities such as Jerry Hall and Jane Seymour in their defence but we must accept that they have the finances to ensure they keep looking good — the rest of us aren't so fortunate. Long hair can be extremely aging, for both men and women on the wrong side of 45. So whether it's a drastic new cut or blonde highlights, go for something different — especially if you've been keeping your hair long for him or her. Lank, greasy hair does nothing for anyone.

Is your personal hygiene up to standard?

This isn't a question of: do you smell? It's more a general assessment of whether you still pay attention keeping hands and fingernails looking nice. Do you regularly remove body hair and keep your underwear in good repair? Metabolism can also alter the smell of favourite perfumes, after shaves, etc., so make sure that you're not clinging to an over-powering fragrance that, combined with the natural acids in your skin, may suggest paint stripper. A new perfume or cologne can be almost as satisfying as a new hair cut but choose wisely. And on the subject of smells — bad breath can stop romance dead in its tracks.

Is your overall, personal appearance outdated?

Women:

Are you wearing skirts too short for your age? There are quite a number of 'women of a certain age' who still enjoy wearing tartytrotters, i.e. 4 inch stiletto heels, using the argument that they still feel smarter when going somewhere special. The combination of high heels and short skirts, however, are best left to the 20-30 somethings with elegance being the province of the older woman. Alternatively, are you still clinging to the Earth Mother regalia or squeezing yourself into jeans as the Big 5-0 looms closer? Is your age or shape conducive to wearing skimpy tops and shorts to the supermarket?

Men:

Does your beard make you look much older than your true age? The majority of women currently find a beard a turn-off — although older women still seem to find them attractive. Women also appear to have a 'thing' about men's socks, the biggest turn-off being white socks, or those which don't bridge the gap between trouser and shoe. Although the tide is beginning to turn and men are being seen more and more out in the shopping malls, older males are not always known for their sartorial elegance. Is it time for you to abandon the 'medallion man' image in favour of something smarter and remember that an out-dated appearance gives the impression of someone clinging onto their lost youth.

So now is the time to opt for a total reinvention and head straight for Weightwatchers, or the local gym to shed those superfluous pounds. Review your wardrobe with a critical eye. Change your hair style and who knows, you may even put a sparkle back into your relationship – if it's not too late.

REALISING A DREAM

We all need something to strive for; some personal goal, ambition or dream that we can work towards. If you've always wanted to take a degree course but never had the time or opportunity for further education, now may be the time to explore the possibilities. It may be that you had to give up a promising career when the children came along; or that overseas promotion was out of the question because it meant leaving the family behind.

One of the most important issues attached to rebuilding your life after a divorce is the decision you make concerning the work-place. One of the most frequently asked questions these days at any social function is: "What do you do?" Because of the competitive structure in our society and although we might not like to admit it, we have become a society in which people are judged not by who they are, but by what they achieve. In other words: a society of winners and losers. This has nothing to do with the old class system; this is a *new class system* created in the 1990s when the goalposts of social values began to shift.

If we don't feel good about our work, then it will have a tremendous impact upon how we feel about ourselves. It may be time for change but it is important to have a clear perspective about what you want to achieve. You may be in a high-powered executive position but now that you've on your own, it may all seem to have been a waste of time, especially if you will be paying out exorbitant amounts of money to keep the family in the marital home.

Conversely you may have nothing left once the lawyer's bill has been paid. Your decision about any future plans will, however, be governed by a several issues:

- financial security or necessity
- a desire to widen a circle of contacts and/or friends
- to resume a career
- the wish to follow a different career or further education
- develop skills or interests which have been impractical until now
- taking the opportunity to do something new and exciting
- to fulfil a need to be needed

The intake for most colleges is usually completed by September and so you may have to tread water until the following year before your enrolment can be accepted. Until recently, there were hundreds of opportunities for mature students in 'further education' but government cut-backs have reduced these quite considerably. You'll need to take your time to find out what courses are now on offer, whether you are eligible for enrolment and what grants may be available to you.

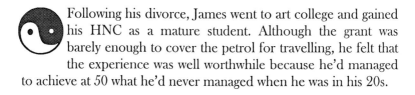 Following his divorce, James went to art college and gained his HNC as a mature student. Although the grant was barely enough to cover the petrol for travelling, he felt that the experience was well worthwhile because he'd managed to achieve at 50 what he'd never managed when he was in his 20s.

The caring professions always need trained staff and even if you don't qualify as a nurse, there are plenty of other posts where you can be useful. Adult students often manage to obtain places on all sorts of study courses, so don't be afraid to ask — simply because it's never too late to work towards a dream.

WHEN IN DOUBT... JOIN SOMETHING

Many find they had to give up sporting interests or hobbies because their partner objected. Unless there is a shared interest, women generally have difficulty in understanding men's preoccupation to sport and this obsession is frequently cited as 'unreasonable behaviour' in divorce cases. Because women are willing to relinquish *their* hobbies or interests when they get married, they (unwisely perhaps) expect men to do the same.

Nevertheless resuming sports and hobbies can be the life-line you need in the event of divorce, simply because you'll be meeting and mixing with people with whom you have a common bond, without the need to form 'relationships'. This is a safe arena whereby you no longer require your partner's approval or have to cope with their disapproval of the other members involved.

Ros had been a reasonably skilled horsewoman before her marriage but Dan resented the time she spent with the horses and eventually they were sold. After the divorce, Ros picked up the reins again for dressage. Her instructor was also divorced and they struck up a friendship based on a mutual regard for horses and a sense of friendly rivalry – 12 months later they married.

William was a school-boy chess champion and still enjoyed a regular game with a friend – until he married Sylvia. She couldn't understand his pleasure in sitting for hours in silence over a chessboard and resented the one evening every week he spent with his childhood friend. Eventually her fussing and fuming forced William to give up chess, although for years they never did anything on his 'chess evening' other than watch the television in silence. Since the divorce William now plays three times a week with different partners and confesses that he's hardly missed Sylvia at all!

From now on you call the shots and thereby take control of another area of your life. Just don't expect to resume a sporting interest or hobby at competitive level if you've been absent for a number of years – just work yourself back in gradually.

NEW HORIZONS

If you have not been in the position of having to go out and make new friends or apply for a job interview for some time, it is quite normal to experience doubts or suddenly experience a total collapse of confidence. It is not easy to join a sports club and be the 'new kid on the block' if you don't have a regular partner for squash or badminton. Most leisure centres are now multi-purpose so even if you can't find a game to join, you can always have a swim instead, or a session in the sauna.

Taking control means making decisions; you either decide to sit at home in isolation or you do something about it. Even the most introverted of us need people now and again, even if we only remain on the fringes of the party. This is where you start to work towards those goals and developing those latent talents. We need to exorcise the false and outdated views we have of ourselves and accept that we have a positive future ahead of us.

Therefore we need to learn about the importance of the 3Rs:

❖ Revising the past

❖ Revitalising the present

❖ Redirecting the future

Learning to live with the knowledge that we *may* have contributed to the failure of our own marriage is our way of revising the past — even if we only admit it privately to ourselves. This doesn't mean that we necessarily regret the separation from a partner but it may help to have a clearer view so that we are no longer quite so one-sided about how we view the past.

As Frances Wilks observes in *Intelligent Emotion,* "It opens us to our compassion and our empathy — not only to others, but also to the wounded part of ourselves." This process helps revitalise ambitions for what we want to achieve in our lives in the here and now and, with the benefit of hindsight , enables us to channel only positive energy towards the future.

WHERE *DID* IT GO WRONG?

In Chapter One we looked at a wide selection of 'compound issues' that, added together, may have contributed to the break-up of your marriage. These were, of course, an over simplification to allow a margin of 'justification' to enter the equation because very few people are willing to admit that there is any fault to be found in their own behaviour. Since it isn't possible to go to a lawyer holding up your hands and saying, "The fault is entirely mine but can I have a divorce, please?" - it is still necessary to provide evidence of your partner's appalling behaviour.

Unfortunately, by the time things get to court, we may even have convinced ourselves that the 'grounds' were genuine, since these allow us to save face in the outside world. After all, we petitioned for a divorce, so we *must* be the innocent party. As we've seen, women instigate 70% of divorce petitions and only a small percentage of these are the result of adultery. That's a lot of bad behaviour that appears to follow a national trend of petitioning for divorce after the family holidays at Christmas and the school summer break.

"My ex- had always been thoughtless," said Gabrielle, "but the real crunch came when the first exhibition of my paintings was arranged at a local gallery. My copy of the catalogue arrived from the publisher and I went into his office to show him. He took it, looked at it, grunted and never mentioned it again. I can still remember sitting on the bottom of the stairs crying because there was no one with whom I could share the moment. By the time my fourth exhibition was staged, he'd gone but I could hardly give my reasons as 'He didn't make enough fuss over my work, your Honour'."

Despite the proclamations from Government and Church, children *aren't* always a blessing in marriage and, rather than bringing stability can have the opposite effect. In a study compiled by *Mother & Baby* magazine, the overall findings were that having a baby could ruin your sex life, marriage and career. Ninety per cent of mothers over 34 said that their relationship *had* been adversely affected by the birth.

A spokesman for the National Family & Parenting Institute said, "Having a baby changes the way women think about themselves. They view themselves more as a parent than as a partner, and this can have a huge impact on a relationship."

 Richard and his wife were delighted at the birth of their son but his wife's resentment at no longer being involved in the day to day running of their business, soon brought problems which eventually culminated in divorce.

The *Mother & Baby* survey also shattered the myth that 21st century males had abandoned their macho attitudes and become more willing to be more involved with raising their children. It is possibly safe to say that three decades of feminism has not emasculated the male of the species as much as they would like to think. The publicity survey carried out to promoted Germaine Greer's book, *The Whole Woman*, showed that 'women regard their men as being domestically useless as ever'.

Learning from the past
Understanding the deeper issues leading to a divorce is a positive way of helping yourself to move on and this is not an easy thing to do. When we begin to take responsibility for our own actions and choices, it is the first step in learning from the problems thrown up by the divorce process. One of the most important lessons is realising just how much the past can interfere with the present if the issues of blame and guilt are not correctly apportioned.

If we are looking at blame and guilt, a survey conducted by now defunct *Vive* magazine, showed that more than a third of divorcees experienced the first little niggling doubts at the altar. In fact, nearly four in 10 people admitted they had doubts about their partners while walking up the aisle but were too far into the commitment to do anything about it.

So were these marriages merely divorces waiting to happen?

REDEFINING RELATIONSHIPS

If anything you miss about being married, it's more than likely to be the companionship of having someone else around the house, and the regular routine that made up a larger part of your social life. Revitalising the present also means taking an often cynical and open-minded view of the people with whom you will continue to have a relationship – and this is not always as easy as it sounds.

Family

Your own family may not be too much of a problem once the dust has settled but there's often resentment simmering under the surface if they feel they're missing out as a result of your divorce. Resentful siblings can soon let you know how much they miss the trips to your holiday villa, irrespective of the fact that your brother-in-law always maintained he couldn't stick your ex- at any price while you were still married. And you father will comment every Christmas that your ex- always gave him a year's supply of 15 year old malt whisky – knowing full well that you can't afford it.

Children

As we've mentioned in Chapter Four, children can be extremely mercenary when it comes to pitting parents against each other. If you're sensible you won't fall victim to the expensive gifts power-play even if you find that your ex's new girl/boyfriend is fuelling the situation. Sit it out and try not to let it get to you – this is 'situation normal', as hundred of divorced parents with children of all ages will tell you.

Parents in law

This is often a tricky one because, after all, they are the grand-parents, too and it's only natural that parents will side with their own child, regardless of who instigated or caused the divorce in the first place. Needless to say, the power-play will be used to good effect here in terms of allowing the children to do exactly as they please, if only to score points over your own parents. If you've got on well with your parent's-in-law, it can also be devastating for them if you suddenly cut off all communication for no other reason than you've ceased to be married to their son or daughter. There may be the situation, of course, that your ex- doesn't wish you to keep in touch with their parents, particularly if there is a new partner in the offing. Discretion is required here but don't be bullied into giving up friendships if they are important to you.

Friends

We've also discussed in Chapter 5 how so-called friends can let you down, so be careful what you say in front of those who have remained on good terms with you both. It is rare that this sort of relationship can continue for any length of time and, like family, they will come down in favour of one or the other eventually. The telling time often comes when you and/or your ex- meet someone new or re-marry — the balance of the scales will be tipped by how much your friends take to your or your ex's new partner.

CAN'T HELP LOVIN' THAT MAN ...

A surprising number of ex-wives find themselves having sex with their former husbands, even when the dust has settled after the divorce.

 Karen has a 'regular arrangement' with her ex- despite the fact that they've been divorced for four years and he's now married to someone else. "It's safe sex," she admits. "The prospect of starting a sexual relationship with a new lover I find quite frightening. The body's not as good as it was and at least my ex- knows what to expect under the duvet."

But doesn't it bother him that he's being unfaithful to his second wife? "He takes the attitude that as we've been married, it's not as though he's committing adultery. I don't want him back, so I'm no threat the new wife."

 Margaret is also loath to expose the scars of several operations to a new man. "I'd be too embarrassed to take my clothes off. My ex- doesn't take any notice, he's seen them all before."

The *Vive* survey also revealed that 11% of divorcees had sex with their former partner, and 10% went on holiday together since they split up. One per cent remarried their former partner, while 17% maintained they would still consider doing so.

THERE'S A WHOLE NEW WORLD OUT THERE
To enable you to move on, you must learn to let go of the past. That said, moving on after a broken long-term relationship can be easier said than done, especially if you still harbour strong feelings for your former husband or wife. It is also extremely hard to come to terms with the fact that the person to whom you were married for many years has re-married and re-built their lives with someone else.

VIEWPOINTS FROM THE LAYMAN'S ARMS
Following the breakdown of the family business and subsequent divorce, Jane found herself in a rather unexpected position. On visiting the local Jobcentre for advice, she discovered that because she had more than £8,000 savings she was not entitled to claim any benefits (which she didn't want) but because she wasn't receiving any benefits, she wasn't eligible to apply for any government retraining schemes. Having helped run the family business she had good administrative and computer skills. Acquiring the certificates to prove her worth, however, will cost her money because she isn't eligible for any subsidised government courses. The £8,000, which she wants to keep towards her retirement, has become a liability. Should she accept the 'official' solution that she should spend all her money and then ask for help?

Male response:
"No. She should hide her savings and lie! She's not asking anything from the State other than to get on her feet to be able to earn."

"No. She should argue that any monies in her account be regarded as a redundancy payment in lieu of notice, which does not debar her from 'benefits'."

Female response:
"No. She should hide all her money in separate accounts and claim whatever she can get. The law doesn't support people who want to help themselves. It forces you to be dishonest."

"Personally, I would put the savings in an account in my mother's name and claim benefit. Since she has worked to save the money towards her retirement, why should she have to use it when she is perfectly willing to continue to work to support herself?"

"So that ends my first experience with matrimony, which I always thought a highly overrated performance."

Isadora Duncan

Chapter Nine

Rebuilding the new you

When you look at ways of re-building your life after divorce, one of the most sensible starting points is obviously diet because we are what we eat. What we may not realise is that a large number of common ailments can be caused by deficiencies in our diet. Feeling listless and run down can be due to a lack of exercise, sleep or anxiety (especially following a divorce) but, more often than not it's because we may be eating the wrong kind of food.

Before the divorce you may have been working full time and, often with a family to consider, probably sat down to your main meal in the evening when everyone was at home. Now may be a good time to look at what you eat and whether a change in diet might make you fitter and healthier. A British Social Attitudes survey showed that 86% of adults had made an effort to change to a healthier diet during the past ten years. Of these, 57% claimed to have cut down on sugar; 56% grilled rather than fried food; 56% ate more wholemeal bread; 37% had cut down on processed meats, and 27% ate more fruit and vegetables. Although on the surface, these figures point to a healthier awareness, it was estimated that ready prepared or processed foods still made up 75-80% of most people's diets.

FUELLING THE BODY

If your daily diet is providing more calories than are being burned off during the course of your normal daily routine, the remainder will be converted to fat. On the opposite side of the coin, if your normal diet isn't meeting your energy requirements, your body will siphon off any fat that, in turn, could lead to malnutrition.

There is an old adage that: A man should breakfast like a king, lunch like a prince and dine like a pauper. By eating a hearty breakfast and a reasonable lunch, the digestive system can break down the food during your most active part of the day. A heavy meal eaten in the evening, followed by several hours in front of the computer or television means that it may not be completely digested before you go to bed.

A breakfast of cereal and fruit, with either fish or meat, accompanied by potatoes and vegetables/salad for your main meal, means that soup and a sandwich will provide a healthy and balanced diet. Realistically, most people find it difficult to maintain a balanced diet every day of the week but eating fruit, wholemeal biscuits or fresh vegetable in a low-fat dip when you fancy a snack, can help to even things out.

Getting the balance right

The secret of a well balanced diet is to aim at eating the right combination of meals over a three -or four-day period. If you decide to binge on sticky toffee pudding for supper, make sure the next couple of days are low in fat and sugar.

The problem with a regular diet of processed foods is not what is lost in the processing but what *has been added.* Some processed meals tend to be high in unhealthy additives such as salt and sugar. Food preservation methods include adding chemicals, drying, freezing, heating, irradiating, refining and fermenting. Then the food is packed in an assortment of packaging from steel cans, aluminium containers, plastic boxes, to cardboard boxes and cling-film that do not enhance the content.

HOW HEALTHY IS YOUR DIET?

Life would be pretty boring if you couldn't indulge in a fried egg and sausage sandwich, or a sticky toffee pudding, now and again, but does sugar and fried food (and that includes fish and chips) make up a large portion of your weekly diet? Do you:

✓ eat plenty of fresh fruit, vegetables and salad every day?

- ✓ buy vegetables from the supermarket, or from local farmers' market?
- ✓ eat convenience food more than once a week?
- ✓ buy meat from the supermarket, or from a local butcher?
- ✓ buy local, free range eggs?

Whatever our eating habits, a variety of *fresh* vegetables and fruit needs to play a major role in menu planning. Unfortunately, the definition of 'fresh' is impossible to pin down in supermarket parlance. We should take into account that the produce in most shops and supermarkets may not be fresh as we are led to believe, since certain vitamins (notably vitamin C) degrade very quickly during warehousing and transportation.

There is a marked difference between garden-fresh and 'market-fresh' foods and produce sold as 'fresh', may not be as wholesome as it appears. As we can see from the labels, a large amount of fresh fruit is imported and may have spent days, weeks or even months in transit or storage. Frozen fruits and vegetables are the next best thing to home-grown because they are harvested at peak-quality and quick-frozen, thereby retaining nearly all of their food value. In fact, frozen fruit may contain more vitamin C than fresh fruit that has only been stored for a few days.

Buying locally

More and more local food producers are now beginning to sell their produce at Farmer's Markets. It is generally accepted by the organisers that stall holders must have grown, bred, caught, pickled, brewed or baked the produce themselves. The emphasis is on helping local producers and processors to sell their goods direct to the public, near their source of origin, by creating benefits for them and the local community. This system of marketing also places an emphasis on added value, quality and freshness, providing direct contact between customers and producers, so you can be sure how your vegetables are grown and meat produced.

KEEPING HEALTHY

A lack of adequate vitamins and minerals in your daily diet can be a contributing factor for more serious diseases, but by eating plenty of fresh fish, fruit and vegetables, you will probably get all you need from your food. Remember that vitamin deficiency occurs when foods are exposed to light and heat, or cooked in *large* amounts of water. After food is eaten, any beneficial effects of vitamins and minerals also diminishes if certain other substances (such as alcohol, smoking, laxatives or barbiturates) are consumed.

Getting your vitamins

The accumulated evidence from over 300 studies suggests that eating large qualities of foods containing vitamins E, C and beta carotene have a reduced the risk of many different type of cancer, heart disease, cataracts and strokes. Vitamin D. as well as having disease-preventing properties. also helps combat osteoporosis. Fruits and vegetables contain natural substances that enhance the absorption of vitamin C and have other protective properties. It is the food itself that is particularly valuable, not the isolated nutrients that are found in supplements

Sources of Beta Carotene

Orange, red and yellow vegetables and fruits are high in beta carotene and other carotenes that may help to reduce the risk of lung cancer. The fibre in these foods many contribute to a reduced risk of colon cancer.

Sources of Vitamins D and E

Oily fish and fortified cereals are a good source of vitamin D, which helps strengthen bones. Vegetables oils, sunflower seeds and nuts are rich in vitamin E and will help to prevent damage to fatty acids in the body.

Sources of Vitamin C

Citrus fruits, broccoli and potatoes are rich in vitamin C, which is an effective cancer preventer and helps to block the formation of cancer-causing nitrosamines.

Feeding the children

Sensible eating and children aren't always synonymous with each other. (One friend despaired when her son existed for over a year eating nothing else but sausages, chips and beans.) So legislating that a new dietary regime is in progress probably isn't going to have any effect or be met with very much enthusiasm, especially if the family is still reeling from the upheaval of the divorce.

One absent father was requested to provide a full roast dinner whenever his son came to stay because his ex-wife was on a 'rabbit food and nut-cutlet' binge, which his son hated. This eventually led to friction and the accusation that the ex-husband was trying to undermine her control of the boy's health. "I told her where she could stick her raw carrot," said her ex- with some degree of relish.

Tact and compromise is the order of the day and it might just lead to co-operation all the way around. Explain the problems exacerbated by a shortage of time and money; ask for help in planning and preparing weekly menus that everyone will enjoy.

- Get everyone to list their favourite foods, and the thing they like the least.

- Talk about the ingredients for a healthy breakfast and ask for suggestions that are easily put together when everyone is in a hurry.

- Simplify breakfast and packed lunch preparation by planning ahead.

- Make a note of everyone's suggestions for adding healthier foods to the menu and a compromise over which unhealthier foods should be reduced.

- List the favourite foods that are high in sugar and fat and agree when and how frequently these can be added to the menu.

- Think up interesting alternatives for the family's packed lunches that don't contain lots of sugar, fat or additives.

- Suggest that the family tries a new recipe at least once a month

- Encourage children to help in the kitchen and/or with the menu planning.

- Exchange crisps and sweets for healthy snacks, including dried fruits that can compensate for a sweet tooth.

Even if you don't have children to cater for, now is as good a time to introduce a healthy diet for yourself and the ideas listed above can easily be adapted for someone living alone.

REST & RECUPERATION

In military parlance R&R comes after a strenuous tour of duty and divorce is strenuous. It doesn't matter whether you were on the giving or receiving end, you've gone through a minefield of emotions that will have left you mentally and physically exhausted. Like a diamond, life is (or should be) made up of many different facets — none more or less important than the others.

In her book, *Take Time For Your Life*, Cheryl Richardson explained that when we live a more holistic life, we naturally distribute our time and energy differently, "creating a sense of balance that leaves you less vulnerable to crisis when changes occur in one area or another." That way, if we find ourselves facing a divorce, we can fall back on the other parts of our life to support us and the problem no longer takes on life-threatening proportions.

If you have been in a marriage where nearly 80% of your time and energy revolved around the family then the fact that you are no longer part of that family unit *will* feel as though a great void has appeared in your life. Between the stress of fighting and breaking up it is often extremely difficult to concentrate on work or other activities, and many people become obsessive about their ex-partner and/or family and worry continually about living alone. There may also be a sense of bitterness when we stop and reflect on how we've been living our life and how much of that time has been devoted to other people, i.e. a husband/wife and/or children — and for what?

Having begun to implement a healthy diet that should make you feel physically lighter and fitter, it is also important not to neglect the mind. In the weeks and months after a divorce we seem to spend a lot of time on our own so use the time productively to stimulate your mind while you're waiting to get on with your life.

FUELLING THE MIND

Whereas we may not be ready to join the great social whirl, it is important not to allow the mind to atrophy while we're putting all the pieces back together. This is the time to start taking an interest in things outside the home and something to consider is a local reading group. Reading groups are becoming increasingly popular with a staggering 50,000 people involved across England. 69% of the groups are women, and two thirds of the members are more than 40 years old. More than 50% have been in higher education, two thirds are working and, geographically the numbers are higher in rural areas than in towns.

The groups range in size from six to a dozen people, who meet every six weeks or so to discuss the books they have all read, usually a novel or biography. Reading groups are also springing up in the workplace where members meet in their lunch hour to talk about books. If you are of a more solitary nature, Penguin Books have an online reading group to offer a whole range from their contemporary and classic fiction, together with a filmed interview with an author of the month and recommended reading.

Take time out for a good book — even if it's only Harry Potter — and make sure that you give yourself a few hours each week to be able to relax and enjoy it. After all, *when* was the last time you managed to sit down and enjoy reading? If you haven't got one already, call in at your local library and apply for a reader's pass. While you're at it, have a look around to see what's on locally and get yourself on the mailing list of the local arts or leisure centre.

As another check-list, make a note of the things you enjoyed be-fore, or had to give up for your marriage, for example:

- Reading
- Listening to music or going to concerts
- Theatre
- Cinema
- Sporting activities
- Creative arts
- Crafts and hobbies
- Community work

As a starting point, check out the local community theatre and get yourself on their mailing list. An army of volunteers usually run these groups, and if you have an interest in what goes on behind the scenes, it may also be a way of making new friends.

When Sue was divorced, she lived in West London and joined Questors Theatre, doing her stint on 'front of house' duty, showing people to their seats. "Questors Theatre kept me sane," she remembers. "Membership also offered access to the Grapevine Bar and I could call in for a drink, especially over the weekend, and find some good company even if I was on my own. Apart from being one of the best 'amateur' compa-nies around, there's always plenty to do if you have a genuine love for theatre. With a different performance each month and helping out behind the scenes, gives you the best of both worlds."

TAKE TIME FOR YOUR LIFE

Start by re-examining your weekly schedule and re-programming a slot just for you. Without it being a chore or getting in the way of family commitments, how long has it been since you have supper with friends or went to the cinema? When was the last time you set-tle down for a relaxed evening at home with a video or a good book, together with a expensive supper and a bottle of wine? Can you remember the pleasure of going to the gym or visiting an exhibition, without having to rush home? How many social invitations have you turned down because of pressure from work or the family?

- If you have a full time job, study your work-load and see which day of the week allows you to finish regularly at a reasonable hour. Let it be known that you are unavailable after that time, switch off the mobile, and make arrangements to do something relaxing like having a sauna or massage to help you unwind before meeting up with friends for supper, or going home for a relaxed evening. This is your mid-week oasis of calm and it's amazing how rejuvenating a few hours of quality time can be.

- If you are self-employed, take an afternoon off each week. The world will not disintegrate if the mobile is switched off while you work out at the health club. Or use the time to visit the latest exhibition at the local museum or art gallery. Take time to re-connect with the finer things of life.

- Those of you who are single parents you will find it is even more difficult to 'get a life' simply because life always seems to be slipping away. This applies to men as well as women, especially those who are forced to remain at home to look after the children without any family support. Make a concentrated effort to find a babysitter or arrange activities you can share with a friend and their children. Trying to arrange some time off from juggling a job and children may prove to be more difficult but this makes it even more important to free some time for your own pleasure.

Turn to your diary and for the *next three months* block out one evening or afternoon every week that is just for you. First you must become selfish and start to re-arrange your routine to reflect the priorities for getting on with life and meeting people.

REDISCOVERING YOURSELF

Left with time on our hands we often discover that we are no longer the person we thought we were. Marriage (and its subsequent failure), producing children, shifts in career, life-style and environment all go to re-shape the people we once were all those years ago when we first got married. In addition to the obvious physical changes of receding hairlines and increased waistlines, more subtle changes were taking place within our mental and emotional make-up.

Often we've come a long way from the eager young couple who first started out on life's great marital roller-coaster. We may have moved away from our roots due to improved financial circumstances. The passing years may have deprived us of family and friends though dead, illness and migration. Many of us come to realise that the things we'd considered being devastatingly important ten years previously no longer matter. Values change and perspectives shift - and very often it is these barely unperceivable changes that can be the cause of the breakdowns in our relationship.

Once the dust from the divorce has settled we may be surprised to find that we no longer care about the things that have been the driving force in our lives for so long. We no longer want to be one of the millions of people who daily "juggle work and personal obligations trying to get ahead and keep up with the pace of live" — we've done that and where did it get us?

From now on you have a choice about how you're going to live your life; about how you spend you time because we've returned to the subject of keeping control. You can, of course, allow things to rub along hoping they'll eventually sort themselves out — or you can harness up the new you and do something about it!

RELAXATION AND QUALITY TIME

Earlier in the chapter we discussed the importance of taking time out for ourselves so that we can get around to doing the things we seem to have grown out of the habit of doing for one reason or another. It is equally important to have the odd moment of relaxation or quality time at home, too. It might be difficult if you're the parent with care but explain to your children that you require a few moments into which they should not intrude. This is all part of keeping control, and if all else fails — retreat to the bathroom with something nice and smelly, and have a long soak in the bath.

Creating a pleasant atmosphere helps relaxation and soothes the mind. Unfortunately a large number of men dismiss many simple relaxation techniques as being 'girly' and, as a consequence miss out on an effective pick-me-up.

Frank didn't want to be bothered with such rubbish but in humouring a friend who was a self-help trainer found that the ideas weren't so daft after all. "It was the silence in the empty flat that I found unbearable when I came home after work. That was when the divorce really got to me. A friend suggested I put the radio on a timer so there was music playing when I opened the door. We drew up a simple routine that I was to put into operation every evening from the moment I walked in the door:

☺   Change over to favourite music on CD
☺   Pour a large Scotch (or white wine)
☺   Light a perfumed candle or joss stick
☺   Run a deep bath with essential oils
☺   Change into comfortable clothes
☺   Relax for half an hour with glass of Scotch/wine
☺   Prepare a simple supper
☺   Relax with a book, or watch TV/video

"Within a couple of weeks I was really beginning to feel the benefit and felt more relaxed than I'd done for months. Of course, I still miss my family but I don't allow myself to just sit around feeling sorry for myself as soon as I got home from work as I had been doing. Having said that, I wouldn't admit to my mates that I'm using essential oils and candles, they'd think I'd gone New Agey or something."

Whatever we do, it is important to have those few moments each day because we all tend to ignore our emotional 'health' until there's a problem. A surprisingly high number of people suffer from stress, especially the breakdown of a long-term relationship, but until they explore methods of controlling the condition via simple relaxation techniques, the problem will not go away.

SELF-UNDERSTANDING AND SELF-ESTEEM

It's important to accept that a failed marriage doesn't make you a failure. Even the so-called experts can get it wrong as was proved when one of the authors of *The Rules*, the best-selling book of advice for women seeking a husband, filed for divorce from her husband on the grounds of abandonment! Ironically, the news came on the eve of the launch of her latest book, *Rules III*, which carried the sub-title *Time-tested secrets for making your marriage work* - hundreds of advance copies had been sent out trumpeting the happy state of the author's marriage.

One of the most important 'universal truths' is the fact that *everyone* makes mistakes — or as the old saying goes "Show me the man who's never made a mistake, and I'll show you a man [or woman] who's never made anything." There are very few people who can go through life without making a mistake about a relationship, as the present divorce figures testify. So while it's not very nice to be just another statistic, there is some comfort in knowing that you belong to a rapidly expanding community!

Finding a positive viewpoint

Accepting that people (including ourselves) make mistakes over marriage is the first step to approaching the situation from a positive viewpoint rather than a negative one. The divorce process has a strong de-valuing effect on both men and women but until they can get to grips with the idea that their life is every bit as important as anyone else's, attempting to implement any positive changes is extremely difficult.

In *Choosing A Better Life*, the author stresses that: "Valuing yourself is about acknowledging that you are important and that you deserve to have a successful and happy life, If you do not believe this, you cannot expect to achieve it. The biggest problem with most people is that they do not value themselves enough. This causes them to have low self-esteem and to doubt themselves and their worth."

Divorce undermines the self-esteem of even the most confident of people for one very simple reason. Someone who knows us more intimately than anyone else has made this undermining attack on our personal worth. Therefore, we suspect that there must be a grain of truth in the accusations, even if we are evenly matched in trading verbal insults. Divorce *does* bring out the worst in people but the childish insults we hurl at each other can have long-lasting effect if we don't keep them in perspective.

For example:

Sue was informed by her partner, that having reached 50, she'd have difficulty in finding another partner because men of a similar age were only interested in younger women. She was too old and past it.

What her partner really meant was that he was only attracted to younger women and that Sue would be better off staying with him.

James was told he was lousy in bed and that his wife's new lover knew exactly what to do to press all the right buttons.

What his ex-wife really meant was that because she no longer loved him, she no longer found him attractive and didn't want sex with him anymore. Her comments were her 'justification' for going off with another man and shifted the blame onto James.

Anthea was on the receiving end of being left for a younger, slimmer woman because she was "fat and an embarrassment".

What her partner really meant was that he'd fallen out of love with her because he'd met someone new. Anthea no longer bothered with her appearance and was no longer the woman he'd married but again, he found a way of shifting the blame for him having an affair.

Jeremy's boyish sense of humour led him to be accused of being stupid and immature.

What his partner meant was that she'd changed and no longer found him amusing company. His more casual approach to life had become a constant source of irritation and she cited this as his unreasonable behaviour.

In all four cases there was a *grain* of truth but each of those on the receiving end found that their ex-partner' s comments had undermined their confidence in themselves.

Sue *did* believe for a time that she was too old for another relationship until she met Jeff. James *was* afraid of having sex until he found a new lady whom he could talk to about his wife's attack. Anthea really did feel she was 'too fat to live' until she joined Weightwatchers. Jeremy suppressed his love of life until he met someone who didn't find him ridiculous.

Once we understand why our ex-partner has delivered such a devastating body blow in the heat of an argument, it makes it easier to dismiss the self-doubts that creep into the subconscious. (And *please* - don't pretend you've never retaliated with something similar.) The human mind is all about justification and if we can shift the blame on to someone else, it makes it easier to walk away with a clear conscience. If you're contemplating divorce, or just discovered you're on the receiving end of one, try to remember that hanging on to your self-esteem will enable you to take control of the way you approach the problem.

DOWNSHIFTING TO A RICHER LIFE

Taking control also means looking long and hard at the way we live and for the average divorced man and women there won't be a lot of surplus money to spare.

Now is as good a time as any to accept that we cannot turn the clock back and regain a lifestyle that was based on material things if our present income won't stretch to that sort of expenditure. Downshifting means an acceptance of the fact that there's more to life than possessions and, where possible, to get rid of as much clutter as we can – on both the material and emotional levels.

When we have to begin again we often have to make do with our 'share' of the matrimonial home, which may not fit in with the atmosphere we want to create. Feng shui is still one of those fads that has turned into an extremely lucrative business leeching off the housing market - which is a long way from the original interior decorating spin of using a mix of superstition and Eastern mysticism.

In reality, much of what is on offer is plain commonsense when it comes to creating a pleasant, uncluttered atmosphere in a home. The continuing fashion for minimalist décor is something any architect or designer would suggest: to get rid of clutter to achieve the impression of space; put plants and flowers near the front door; let in plenty of fresh air and use mirrors to reflect light.

Like all branches of fashionable mysticism, there is a core of truth in feng shui, so go to the library and take out a couple of books on the subject. Ignore the 'instant harmony' aspects of the content and take on board the *practical* suggestions for improving your home. Give your house or flat a thorough make-over across a three- to six-month period, paying particular attention to the entrance, your bedroom and the sitting room. Clutter should be removed and any large pieces, such as pictures, ornaments and chairs should be arranged in groupings or pairs.

Throwing away the past

As we have said, minimalism is still in and so it might be a good idea to throw away those things that keep you tied to the past and prevent your cupboard doors from closing. Getting rid of superfluous possessions also cuts away a considerable amount of emotional baggage because the memories we take with us to furnish our new home should be pleasant, harmonious ones. Possessions are a constant reminder of what we have been and where we have come from; they represent those obstacles and challenges in life that have brought us to where we stand today. By discarding material things we no longer need, or have outgrown, we can also take the opportunity to jettison outworn attitudes and behaviour in order to make room for a new beginning.

VIEWPOINTS FROM THE LAYMAN'S ARMS

With the changes to the divorce laws insisting that settlements should be based on contributions each party makes not only to the family wealth but also to the bringing up of the family itself, the law does not concern itself with who is to blame for the marriage breakdown. Should there be a 'fair division of wealth' where the person making a claim for a 50/50 split has been instrumental in breaking up the marriage for trivial personal reasons, or where they have played no active part in the actual earning of the wealth?

Male response:

"Not really. 50/50 should only apply if both partners had contributed equally to the marriage, not necessarily in a financial way. Part of the contribution to the marriage should take into account the trying to keep it all together before divorce proceedings are pursued."

"No. It should be based on the wage earner supplying a limited needs allowance."

Female response:

"Lines have to be drawn somewhere and you can't suit all of the people all of the time. A 50/50 split would be fair for the majority of cases."

"I think if the marriage breaks down 50/50 is fair. Although you would feel bitter and probably want to take for all you could get, if you were the injured party."

Chapter Ten

There Is Life After Marriage

Even if you don't particularly believe it at the moment, there *is* life after a failed marriage and, sooner or later, you'll want to climb back onto the world and start all over again. If life wasn't complicated enough in the relationship stakes, however, not a week goes by when researchers from around the world come up with the latest research data to inform us why our relationships work or fail. Nearly every university and social institute in the Western world has something to say on why we behave the way we do and in doing so, puts itself at odds with most members of society.

WHAT THE EXPERTS SAY ...

As the government puts its full support behind marriage by describing it as the "foundation of a strong and stable society", the results of a survey conducted by the Institute for Social & Economic Research was a blow for those who champion family values. According to the findings, one in five people will never get married; while others who are rejecting single life, chose to live with their partners instead.

The survey carried out by *Vive* also revealed that the experience of marriage and divorce hadn't put people off - no fewer than 78% said they'd 'definitely' or 'maybe' get married again. These people were obviously not deterred by the fact that according to the figures from the National Office for Statistics, half of all second marriages will end in divorce and nearly 60% of third marriages fail.

A report published in the *New Scientist* claims that the secret of a long and faithful marriage is to marry a short man. According to American and German scientists, tall men are more likely to divorce and remarry, usually replacing the first wife with a woman who is at least two years younger and better educated. The simple reason being that taller men had more opportunities to stray than their shorter counterparts and twice as many tall men as short men divorced and remarried. On average, taller men were also evaluated more favourably by women.

The *New Scientist* also reported that according to researchers in Holland and Sweden, in relationships women stay with men for security, and men remain with women for sex.

Avoiding the same trap

All of which tells us that if we listen to the 'experts', we'd never form a successful relationship ever again and expect it to last. What we do need to be on guard against is:

    i.   Making the same mistake again
    ii.   Forming a 'rebound' relationship
    iii.   Rushing into another relationship

It's been illustrated over and over again that women in particular, are attracted to the same type of man and, as a result, may find that they find history repeating itself. This isn't to say that all men and women of a certain type will batter their wives, or that Rod Stewart ought to give up on blondes, but the tell-tail signs are there and we must be on our guard against falling into the same trap.

Forming a relationship before the pain and hurt of the last one has been dealt with is asking for trouble. This is often the case of transferring all your suspicions or fears onto the new (wo)man in your life who, as a result of these premature signs of possessiveness, will back off, increasing the level of pain and hurt on being 'let down' once again. Like a broken arm, all mental/emotional injury needs time to heal before you can expect to cope with the stresses and strain of new relationships.

Some people, on the other hand, cannot bear to be alone and find themselves in another relationship before the sheets have had time to cool. This is not a question of loose morals but an on-going problem of insecurity. Unfortunately, it means that this person does not give themselves time to adjust to reverting to a single status and taking life as it comes. They have a pressing need to be protected/cared for and often find themselves pitched back into another doomed relationship.

HAVING FUN

Learning to enjoy life again as a single person means that we can expand our circle of friends without the complications of romantic entanglement. In *Intelligent Emotion*, Frances Wilks defines the differences between joy and happiness - and learning to rebuild our lives means that we should not confuse the two. "Joy is inner-directed and independent, happiness is outer-directed and de-pendent. We need both," writes Frances Wilks, "Joy shows us our creative and transformative potential while happiness connects us in relationships to people and things in the world."

Just because we've suffered deep emotional hurt as a result of our partner's defection, doesn't mean that we will ever stop longing for people and things that make us happy. This is a recognised part of the human condition and by taking control of where we want to go at this stage of our lives means that cultivating a joyful approach to the future will often make the quest for happiness more fun and much more light-hearted. "Happiness is an all-or-nothing thing and can so easily be marred by one thing going wrong," continues Frances Wilks. "if we are attuned to joy rather than happiness, then we won't regard things going wrong destruc-tively."

Pursuing happiness

When we're emotionally upset everything is seen from a nega-tive standpoint and it is often extremely difficult to shake off this downward spiral. A divorce can appear to offer no bright hope for the future and by denying the reality of our present situation (abandoned/cast out) we are also veiling the issues about past cir-cumstances that led to it. We need to begin a pursuit of happiness starting with the simple pleasures in life and by making time for ourselves.

Of course it isn't possible to switch to instant 'having fun' mode but fun is an essential ingredient in our lives because it has a positive impact on our general health and well-being. When people find themselves in a position of intense emotional upheaval as a result of divorce or bereavement, however, they tend to take the attitude that any demonstration of being fun-loving is unseemly behaviour. There's nothing in the rules to say that we can't enjoy life to the best of our ability and we may need to re-examine the underlying expectations of our social grouping and ask ourselves whether we agree with them.

If you have a dream don't let anyone tell you that you are:

- too old
- not old enough
- not fit enough
- not qualified
- too qualified
- foolish

to pursue whatever it is that you feel will make you happy. After all, it's rather a sad person who puts away all childish things forever — so go out and have fun!

FROM NEW BEGINNINGS

Making a fresh start is always rather frightening — if we turn the clock right the way back to our first day at school, we can probably still taste the fear generated by this particular rite of passage. New beginnings mean leaving things behind and moving on. The need to move on may not have been of our choosing but like a lot of things in life, when we've been thrown a curved ball the best thing we can do is go out to meet the challenge and give it our best shot.

Because you made the decision quite early on in the divorce stakes to take control of your life, you will (hopefully) have reached the stage where you feel you can plan your future the way you want it. By balancing all the different areas that make up your new life-style the field is open for all sorts of different enterprises, especially if you no longer have any regular family commitments. As we've discussed before, your life is *yours* to control. Other people, such as children, ex-partners, family and friends may have some degree of influence over certain restricted areas but what you do with the way you spend your time is entirely up to you.

Making changes

As Jones and Gilbert write in *Choosing A Better Life*: "If you are not happy with your life at the moment, or if you think some or all of it could be better, it's up to you to take the responsibility for do-ing something about it. Don't blame other people if you make the wrong choices, or if you aren't prepared to take personal responsi-bility for making changes."

Making changes means exercising control over the way you balance your life between work and leisure activities. It also means that you do not feel guilty about the way you spend your own leisure time "like taking a full lunch hour or spending a quiet half hour reading the newspaper. This may entail asking someone else for their help, perhaps changing your job so that it fits in with what you want to do, or spending less time at work so that you can have more quality time" for making new friends and socialising

"MIDDLE-AGED DIVORCEE SEEKS ..."

The difficulties of meeting suitable people of the opposite sex has turned 'dating facilities' from a bit of a sad joke to a much more widely accepted method of finding a prospective partner. In the early days, dating agencies were looked upon as the last resort of the desperate, but as *WLTM: The Dating Game* points out, nowa-days they can be found in nearly every newspaper and magazine in the country. With the onset of technology, there has been a marked increase in the number of telephone introductory services that allow you to hear the voice message of a potential 'date' before making any contact.

According to a recent survey, one in five people now use dating agencies to find a friend or potential partner, and that figure is expected to double over the next five years. Be warned, however, that anyone can set themselves up as a dating agency and although there are organisations such as the Association of British Introduction Agencies and the Introduction Services Federation, neither have any legal clout and the fraudsters are having a field day.

Dating facilities have dozens of different outlets from the traditional dating agency through lonely-hearts columns, box numbers, telephone ads, singles clubs, holidays, the Internet and text messaging ranging from £7,000 (for an 18 month membership) to free online. There are now dating agencies for Christian, Hindu, Muslim or Jewish folk if religion is an obstacle to meeting Mister or Miss/Ms Right. Even some supermarkets have introduced a 'Singles Nights'!

- So which to chose?
- Why should you want to consider the idea in the first place?

According to *WLTM: The Dating Game*, the older we get the less opportunities there are for meeting unattached people of the opposite sex. A 45+ divorcee doesn't want to go trailing round the town's wine bars, being chatted up by a strange of assortment of predatory males. The 50+ male can no longer hang out in the local dance hail as he did in his youth because they no longer exist — and he's run out of practice with the chat-up line. For the older man and woman such behaviour is degrading and embarrassing but neither can they rely on their friends to introduce them to a suitable dinner-date because unattached people of a 'certain age' appear to be extremely thin on the ground. Despite the divorce figures running at around 155,000 per year (that's 310,000 individuals back in circulation every twelve months) the intriguing question as to where they go once they hit singledom again is almost as unanswerable as 'Where do flies go in winter?'

Having said that, for all those newly single women around the 50 mark, there is a single man looking for companionship and/or romance. Older singles tend to be more discriminating and won't rush into a relationship; they know the sort of person they like and they are not prepared to put up with second best. Many are prepared to put in a lot of effort to make new friends — much to the embarrassment of their adult children.

One chap spent several years going on cruises and singles' holidays — he met his new wife at a *local* singles club and discovered she only lived a couple of streets away. He was attracted to her because she never asked what he did, or what type of car he drove.

"The word 'suitable' sounds awfully snobbish," says Sue, "but I've been introduced to more unsuitable men by well-meaning friends than I care to admit. Some have been exceptionally nice but I never get the opportunity to meet the kind of man with whom I'm at ease because my work keeps me on the move. Since my divorce, I've met very few unattached men and I've been considering using a dating agency for some time."

Choosing the right method

Perhaps the secret of deciding which method to choose is down to 'market research' and finances. If you can afford the fees or have an income that allows for weekend breaks and overseas holidays, there are a growing number of organisations like Nexus that cater for singles of all ages, where the emphasis is on making new friends rather than dating. The Internet give even greater access to organisations such as Friends United, who puts you in touch with old friends, while offering the opportunity to make new ones. Agencies such as Just Woodland Friends and Attractive Partners provide the more traditional dating services for a reasonable fee.

Jackie tried computer dating and filled in all the relevant boxes but her first date turned out to be a complete disaster. "I'm vegetarian and belonged to the anti-hunt lobby. My date turned out to be a Master of Foxhounds! We'd both ticked 'countryside and conservation'. Fortunately, we were both civilised enough to see the funny side but the meeting could have had serious repercussions."

Telephone personal ads are becoming increasingly popular since these can give a rough indication of an advertiser's outlook and/or politics. The newspaper or magazine is aimed at an identifiable readership and so the advertiser is going to be the average type of reader for that particular publication – unless his sister or secretary has placed the ad! You phone the number given, followed by the ad number and you can hear the voice of the man or woman whom you may wish to meet; if you like what you hear you can leave your telephone number and a brief message.

For example, the majority of Kindred Spirits advertisements in the *Daily Telegraph* will more than likely have been placed by people who are regular readers of that particular broadsheet. An advertisement placed in a local free-paper will tell you nothing about the person placing it because free papers are delivered to every house within the area of circulation. Ads placed in specialist interest magazines will cater for those who wish to meet someone who shares their hobby or sport.

When considering using any of the 'dating facilities, it is important not to pitch your hopes too high. Enter into the spirit of thing with the idea that you're more likely to make friends rather than launching yourself into a torrid love affair with the man of your dreams. Also respect the fact that the majority of those seeking a friend or companion are sincere people – also bear in mind that the dating game also has its fair share of lulus!

GOING ON THE FIRST DATE

Whatever our age, there are a few 'rules' we should observe when making or accepting a date, especially if we haven't done this sort of thing for a long time.

- Arrange to meet your date in a public place, e.g. restaurants, pubs, etc., not at your own home.

- Trust your instincts and don't meet again if you have any doubts.

- On your first date it is best to make your own way to and from the venue.

- It is best not to accept an offer of transport.

- Leave details of your meeting with family or friends when seeing someone for the first time.

- Take your mobile but keep it switched off.

- These points may seem over cautious, but if the person you meet is genuine, they will understand.

Out of consideration for the other's pocket, suggest that the date takes place in an informal setting rather than an expensive restaurant. A lunchtime meeting offers the opportunity for escape if one of you has the need to beat a hasty retreat without giving or taking offence. A lunchtime meeting can be cut short whereas with an evening 'date' isn't quite so easy to escape from if the going gets rough.

Do's and Don't's

Establish whether your date is a smoker or non-smoker since this is a big turn-off these days and could well be the end of a beautiful friendship before you get off first base. Don't over-dress: if you're meeting for an informal meal or drink, it's inadvisable to get 'kitted-up' for Ascot, it will embarrass your companion. Do make an effort to look clean and tidy, otherwise you'll give the impression that you couldn't be bothered to make an effort. Do give some pertinent information about yourself but don't monopolise the conversation. Show a polite interest in your date's occupation. Don't launch into a full-scale self-promotion campaign unless you want your date to go cross-eyed with boredom. Switch off your mobile and if you need to make a call, make your excuses and go to the lobby or cloakroom.

Below is a 'top 10' listing of things that will guarantee you don't get a second date.

Top 10 Turn-offs for Him
✗ Low cut or revealing clothes
✗ Bitten fingernails
✗ Poor table manners
✗ Cheap perfume
✗ Tattoos and body piercing
✗ Talking about ex-lovers
✗ Flirting with the waiter
✗ Bad language
✗ A lack of humour
✗ Raucous laughter

Top Ten Turn-offs for Her
✗ Dirty fingernails
✗ Conceit and arrogance
✗ Trying to impress over possessions/career   1
✗ White socks
✗ Double entendre and innuendo
✗ Overpowering aftershave
✗ Body odour
✗ Personal anatomical references
✗ Parsimony
✗ Using a napkin to blow the nose

You may not have done this for a long time but when in doubt fall back on good, old-fashioned common sense and good manners — even if your date turns out to have little of either. Don't look upon a new date as a possible, future partner otherwise you may miss out on friendship, which is equally as important when rebuilding your life. The wider your circle of friends, the less likely you are to rush into a new relationship. If you don't want to see the person again (for whatever reason) try to be as tactful as possible. They have more than likely come from a broken relationship themselves and a unfeeling brush-off won't help their self esteem, even if they did bore you rigid all evening. Most people deserve a little kindness but don't invite them in for coffee!

NEW RELATIONSHIPS AND RE-MARRIAGE

There's an indefinable stage in a relationship where two people change from being 'just good friends' to being 'an item'. This stage can take weeks, months or even years before you get around to admitting that you really would like to take things a step (or leap) forward. Depending on your age and/or inclination, this is also where the subject of sex will enter into the equation, so as the Boy Scout motto says: Be prepared! In the good old days this meant 'A bob (shilling), a penknife and a bit of string'. Today it can be liberally interpreted as 'A flyer (emergency taxi fare), a Swiss army knife and a condom'. Sorry, but just because you've hit middle-age does not meant that sex is safe.

If you're part of the 'Pill generation' you may still think that STD refers to 'state time and duration' for a telephone call – it means sexually transmitted diseases. Safe sex today isn't about getting pregnant, it's all about not catching something nasty that you might not be able to get rid of. It also means that the 'Pill generation' need to familiarise themselves with condom etiquette. It is now considered perfectly normal for women to carry condoms, so if the pace is hotting up in your new relationship, it's quite acceptable for you *both* to be prepared.

When is the time right? When the time is right, so don't push/ get pushed into going to bed with someone because you didn't like to refuse. Unless you've both been out on the dating scene for a while, the odds are evens that you'll both be as nervous as hell about making the first move. There aren't any set rules and the best thing that can be said about advice is: *don't give it!*

Considering marriage

If the relationship gets to the stage of marriage rearing its head, then you'll both need sidestep the romance to do some serious talking about those small, extraneous details like:

- his place or yours
- children
- pets
- an excess of furniture
- wardrobe space

Where you are going to live can depend on how many children you have between you and who has the largest property. Your choice may also be influenced by where you work. If yours is the spare property consider letting it rather than selling because a) you'll have a bolt hole if it all goes wrong, b) it will give you an income, c) it will provide a better return than most investments while increasing in value and d) it will be part of your estate to be left to your children who might otherwise miss out from a second marriage.

Children

can present the biggest problem of all if you don't set the parameters before you start. Resist the urge to pull rank and adopt the 'do as I say' routine since this is guaranteed to alienate stepchildren quicker than anything else, especially if they are teenagers. Be prepared for difficulties and long silences and don't try to force a step-parent onto them. If everyone gives each other enough 'space' then sooner or later they'll come around. Remember children also carry the hurt of divorce for a long time and if you're the interloper then you can't expect them to greet you with open arms. The heavy-handed step-parent will only inherit trouble, so discuss the situation fully with your intended *before* you move in.

Pets

If your prospective partner likes your dog or cat and vice versa ... fine. Discuss whether there will be any restrictions on where the animals can go and where they can't. If you both own a dog, introduce them gradually by taking them for walks together and visiting each other's home. Don't wait until you've moved before sorting out any problems.

Belongings

When it comes down to furniture and belongings, be prepared to compromise. if you're into cottage antique and your future spouse goes for minimalism, there could be a problem. We all have 'treasures' that we'd never part with so even if you think her mother's dinner service is hideous, or you would cheerfully consign his collection of 30s memorabilia to Oxfam, be prepared for some given and take.

Wardrobe space is *always* a problem. There are never enough drawers and hanging space for an extra person's clothes, so try to find ways of packing out of season items into storage boxes. Go through your wardrobe before you move and be ruthless. If you haven't worn it for years, or you can't get into it — get rid of it.

SAFEGUARDING YOUR ASSETS

Although critics (usually female) claim that pre-nuptial agreements are a kiss of death to a marriage, those who contemplate this blissful union for the second time should seriously consider their position before tying the knot. With the statistics for second marriages being no better than the life expectancy of the first, it is in everyone's best interests to apply a bit of common sense.

For example:

£ Some financial advisors claim that if the law is to insist that all assets are split down the middle in the event of divorce, then you might as well run your investments that way from day one of the marriage.

£ Where it is necessary to protect assets gained from the first marriage and to ensure that any children do not lose out in the event of the second marriage breaking up, a pre-nuptial agreement is an ideal solution.

£ Where a wealthy person re-marries someone with considerably fewer financial resources and wants to protect their assets for any children of the first marriage, some formal agreement would solve any long-term problems.

£ Providing there has been a full disclosure of assets before any pre-nuptial agreement is signed and both parties have had separate legal representation, the court is less likely to overturn the arrangement, especially where it safe guards the interests of any children.

If you have children from a previous marriage, or you've reached an age where you and your new partner are unlikely to have any more but you have assets you wish to protect in the event of a second divorce, then consult a solicitor *before* you remarry.

When buying a new home together, it may be advisable to purchase the property not in joint names, but as 'tenants in common', especially if you are co-habiting. This will be officially recorded at the Land Registry that each party owns a portion of the property in their own right. In addition, an equity share deed should be drawn up whereby a split in the value of the home can be established in proportion to the equity contributed to the original purchase.

This prevents problems from arising when the property is sold in the event of death and the proportion passes to the children. Needless to say, it is important for you both to make out a will at the same time since on death your assets will normally pass to your next of kin if you and your partner are not married. Leaving your share of the property to your partner for his or her lifetime can circumnavigate any difficulties arising from avaricious offspring.

THERE'S NO FOOL LIKE AN OLD FOOL

As many have found to their cost, when they fall for someone many years their junior – it more often than not will eventually ends in tears. A British charity worker who fell in love and married a Gambian guide 20 years her junior soon discovered that the romance of the bush couldn't be uprooted and moved to Middle

England. Seven months after the ceremony, she was seeking a divorce because she claims her husband changed drastically after the wedding and that he is not the man she married.

It is not unusual, however, for divorced men and women to be attracted by much younger people for a variety of reasons. The main one being that it makes them feel that they've recaptured their own youth; boosting ego and self-esteem to be seen out with a younger companion. What many fail to realise is that it often makes them appear pathetic, especially if they make no bones about doting on their companion in public.

Chris, aged 53, has no qualms about being seen out and about with a 25-year old graduate. "Okay, so it probably won't last," he says, "but I look on her as a bonus in life and I'll enjoy her company for as long as I can. I don't find 50-year old women attractive."

Tony, now 58, was divorced from his wife of 24 years, following the discovery of an affair. Instead of marrying his lover of a similar age, he met 28-year old Kim and they are now married with a baby daughter. "It was no contest really," he said when asked how he chose between the two women.

Hilary moved to a completely different part of the country following her divorce, where she met Frankie, thirteen year her junior. "Of course the age difference worried me at first," she admitted, "but we're celebrating our twelfth wedding anniversary next year."

This isn't to say that marriage with a younger person is doomed to failure and should be avoided at all costs, since there are thousands of successful relationships that have weathered all sorts of storms and survived. Age is a condition of the mind and if the mind-set of a couple works in harmony then any age gap is immaterial. The problems can arise when the attraction is confined to the physical level where there is no area of compatibility when the novelty wears off.

REDEFINING YOUR GOAL

Having worked our way through all the problems and obstacles that affect divorcing couples, the one thing that must be perfectly obvious – *there isn't a clean and easy way to do it.* Someone is going to be hurt during the process. Whatever the outcome, it is important to re-define the goals you originally set yourself when the idea of divorce first crossed your mind. Much will depends on the reasons why you wish to off-load your partner, or they you.

It is also important to realise that achieving those goals or targets, even in a re-defined form, may still take a lot of hard work. Set yourself targets that you know are realistically within your grasp. After all, there's little point dreaming about becoming an Olympic gold medallist if you've never done anything sporty in your life. Joining a local sports class would be a step in the right direction. We also need to understand that there isn't a seven-point plan we can implement by picking up a book and following the instructions.

If you have no clearly defined goal, or your goal is not realistically achievable, then your life may quickly deteriorate in a succession of missed opportunities. Granted it is extremely difficult to be positive and upbeat if you've just lost your partner, home and family due to divorce but you'll achieve nothing by bemoaning your lot. As Jones and Gilbert wrote in *Choosing A Better Life:* "The great danger of having no direction, or lacking vision, is that rather than being in the driving seat of your life you can only react to the things and changes that *other people impose on you.*"

When re-defining your goal take the following into account:

❖ Understand the difference between a goal (reality)
   and a dream (fantasy)
❖ Be clear and specific about what you want
❖ Be positive about any obstacles that might get in the way
❖ Is what you are aiming for achievable?
❖ Be just as positive about what you *don't* want

Needless to say, some targets are easier to aim for than others and so there should be some sort of time-frame introduced into your planning. Some may take longer to achieve because of the element of financial management, challenge or preparation. Others might be more realistically approached if there is the opportunity to break them down into stages: short-medium and long-term plans. Each stage should be a self-contained unit so that, should you not be able to reach the long-term target, there isn't a sense of total failure because, as the man said: The best laid schemes of mice and men ...

PAUSE FOR THOUGHT

Hopefully you're a lot wiser about divorce now, than when you first took this book off the shelf. There are still lots of things for you to consider and an initial consultation with a solicitor will clarify exactly where you stand as an individual in the divorce stakes. But before you actually give your permission for him to instigate proceedings, take a moment to reflect on Charlotte's story

"Three years ago, I spent three hours consulting a solicitor about a divorce. The grounds would be my husband's unreasonable behaviour. It was a Friday and as I was leaving, the solicitor asked if he should send a letter instituting proceedings. I said I'd make the final decision over the weekend and ring him on Monday morning.

My husband was in denial about how bad our relationship was. He could not believe that I had taken legal advice. He was convinced I'd made it up to frighten him. He spent the weekend in front of the box watching sport. His attitude reinforced my conviction that I was doing the right thing. I believe nothing is lonelier than marriage between two people who've become strangers.

Monday morning. 10 am. I'm sitting next to the phone and my hand's hovering over the receiver. Hands *can* hover; it's not a cliché. In two minutes or less, I could end seventeen years of marriage. I hesitate, thinking – yet again – about the consequences of the call. I know it would change my life forever. I know that it would impact on our daughter's life and that countless other people – family, friends, colleagues – would also be effected. I imagined a rock hurled into the middle of a vast lake. How far would the ripples extend? How long before they fade? Raw emotion has this effect on me, and inside I was bleeding.

I looked back over nearly twenty years, trying to recall the happiness rather than the hurt; remembering the love rather than the loathing. We had a shared history, but did we have a future? Not if I picked up the phone.

Are you a hundred per cent sure you want to go ahead with this? I asked myself. And the answer was: no. I was maybe one per cent in doubt. It was *that close.* The clincher was a mental picture of my teenage daughter and I spending Christmas in some grotty bedsit. She - waiting for a flying visit from an estranged father who might not call and either way - sobbing herself to sleep. We all deserved another chance.

Five years on, I'd love to say I've never regretted it. But a bed of thorns doesn't become a bed of roses overnight. It's hard work cultivating a good marriage, easy to throw it away. We still argue and we still have a long way to go to get it even near right. Several times I've regretted not making that call but more often than not I'm glad I didn't."

Like any other voluntary rite of passage, the important thing about seeking a divorce is to understand exactly what you want to do and *why* you want to do it. We all act and react according to the circumstances in which we find ourselves at any given time and sometimes we're caught 'between a rock and a hard place' when it would seem we can't do right by accident. The point is, it is not merely that we do, or not do, or say something,. It is *why* we want to take that course and the acceptance and/or responsibility of any repercussions. That is what we mean by 'taking control'.

What this book also shows is that the law is often at odds with what the lay person sees in terms of fairness and morality. The reasons behind wanting a divorce may be wholly justified but, like Charlotte, the fact that you may now have a slightly different perspective may alter the way you look at your marriage.

"What we call the beginning is often the end
And to make an end is to make a beginning
The End is where we start from."
[Little Gidding — T S Elliott]

Glossary of Legal Terms

Absent Parent: the term used to describe the parent who does not live in the same house as the children.

Access: (see Contact)

Acknowledgement of Service: the standard form that accompanies the divorce petition, which the Respondent must sign and return indicating whether they are going to defend it or not.

Adultery: sexual intercourse between a married person and another who is not their spouse while still legally married.

Affidavit: a sworn statement of evidence.

Barrister: a member of the bar whom a solicitor may instruct to advise in complex cases, or to deal with court hearings. Also Counsel. (Advocate in Scottish law)

Child of the Family: the children of the divorcing couple – this may also include stepchildren who have lived with the family.

Clean Break: a settlement where there are no continuing financial responsibilities or obligations.

Co-Habitation: a relationship between a couple living together when unmarried.

Conciliation: (see Mediation)

Consent Order: agreements (especially financial) made between the two parties are not legally binding unless the court makes them into an Order.

Contact: the modern replacement for 'access' that sets out the arrangements for when the absent parent can spend time with the children.

Conveyancing: term for all the legal and administrative procedures involved in transferring ownership of a property.

Co-Respondent: the person named in a divorce petition with whom the former spouse committed adultery. Unless costs are to be claimed from them, it is no longer necessary to name the co-respondent.

Custody: no longer used (see Residence)

Decree Absolute: the final court order that dissolves a marriage.

Decree Nisi: where the court has certified that the marriage can be dissolved after six weeks unless sufficient cause is shown to the contrary.

Divorce: the legal dissolution of a marriage.

Equity: the net value of the property after all debts and expenses have been covered.

Ex Parte: an application made to the court without the other party being notified.

Family Lawyers: solicitors in England and Wales who specialise in family law work.

Injunction: a court order restraining a person from a particular course of action. Often used when dealing with domestic violence. (Interdict in Scottish law)

Joint Tenants: if one of the parties should die, the property would automatically go to the survivor. (see Tenants in Common)

Judicial Separation: a court order confirming that the parties are legally separated as an alternative to divorce. Often used in cases where religious reasons prevent a divorce.

Legal Aid: now called Community Legal Service Fund it provides the facility for paying legal fees for those with limited means.

Litigation: legal proceedings

Maintenance: regular payments for the support of the children and/or a former spouse.

Mediation: a recognised process whereby a third party can assist a divorcing couple to reach agreement by negotiation.

Order: a directive issued by the court that must be obeyed.

Parental Responsibility: refers to the rights and responsibilities of the parent over their children, i.e. religion, education and upbringing. (Parental Rights in Scottish law)

Parent With Care: the parent with whom the child lives.

Party: either of the participants in a divorce case.

Petition: the document that starts the ball rolling and which sets out the full details of the divorce.

Petitioner: the person in England and Wales who begins divorce proceedings. (Pursuer in Scottish law)

Property Adjustment: the power of the court to order the transfer of the property from one spouse to another.

Residence: refers to whom the children will live with.

Respondent: the spouse on whom the petition is served.

Separation Agreement: a record in writing of the agreements made on separation.

Solicitor: a qualified member of the legal profession (also Lawyer)

Statement of Arrangements: a standard form that accompanies the divorce petition in England and Wales confirming the arrangements made for the children.

Tenants in Common: each party having its own specific share in the property.

Unreasonable Behaviour: evidence that a spouse has behaved in such an unreasonable manner that the person cannot reasonably be expected to continue to live with them.

Without Prejudice: enables the parties concerned to concede in negotiation while reserving the right to dispute the point if the matter goes to court.

Useful Addresses & Contacts

African Caribbean Family Mediation Services
(now South London Family Centre)
2&4 St John's Crescent, Brixton, London SW9 7LZ
Tel: 020 7737 2366 — Email: southlondonfamily@yahoo.co.uk

Attractive Partners
The introduction agency for fun loving people of all ages
The Old Coach House, Upper Grove Street, Leamington Spa,
Warwicks CV32 5AN
Tel: 0870 2424212—Website: www.attractivepartners.co.uk

Asian Family Counselling
Suite 51, The Lodge, Windmill Place, 2-4 Windmill Lane,
Southall, Middx UB2 4NJ
Tel: 020 8567 5616 — Email: afcs99@hotmagil.com

The Blue Cross Head Office
Offers help, advice and re-housing of family pets.
Shilton Road, Burford, Oxon OX18 4PF
Tel: 01993 822651 —Website: www.bluecross.org.uk

Consumer Credit Counselling Service
Tel: 0800 138 111 (Scotland - Tel: 0800 138 3328)
Website: www.cccs.co.uk

Divorce Recovery Workshop
National support group for separated and divorcing people of
both sexes and all ages.
Tel: 07000 781889 - Website: www.drw.org.uk

Families Need Fathers
134, Curtain Road, London EC2A 3AR
Tel: 020 7613 5060 — Website: www.fnf.org.uk

Family Lawyers
Details of Family Lawyers in your area can be obtained by calling the Law Society on 0870 606 6575 or see their website: www. lawsociety.org.uk under 'Choosing and using solicitors' and 'Find a solicitor' by typing in your Post Code.

Family Mediators, UK College of
Alexander House, Telephone Avenue, Bristol BS1 4BS
Tel: 0117 904 7223   Website: www.ukcfm.co.uk

Gingerbread
Support group for lone parent families in England and Wales
Adviceline: 0800 018 4318   Website: www.gingerbread.org.uk

The Jewish Marriage Council
23 Ravenshurst Avenue, London NW4 4EE
Tel: 020 8203 6311 — Website: www.jmc-uk.org

Justice 4 Fathers
P O Box 7835, Sudbury CO10 8YT
Tel: 01787 281922   Website: www.fathers-4-justice.org

Just Woodland Friends
A national introduction service for country-minded people.
Tel: 01874 636909   Website: www.justwoodlandfriends.com

The Law Society of England & Wales
113, Chancery Lane, London WC2A 1PL
Tel: 0870 606 6575 — Website: www.lawsociety.org.uk

The Law Society of Northern Ireland
71 3rd Floor Bedford House, 16-22 Bedford Street,
Belfast BT22 7FL Tel: 01232 246441 — Website: www.nilad.org

The Law Society of Scotland
26 Drumsheugh Gardens, Edinburgh EH3 7YR
Tel 0131 226 7411 — Website: www.lawscot.org.uk

Muslim Women's Helpline
Tel: 020 8904 8193 Website: www.mwhl.org

National Association of Farmers' Markets
P O Box 575, Southampton SO15 7BZ
Tel: 0845 4588 420 Website: www.farmersmarkets.net

Nexus
Nexus House, 6 The Quay, Bideford, North Devon EX39 2HW
The largest 'singles' group in the country for those who looking to expand their social lives.
Tel: 01237 471704

The Penguin Readers Group
Website: www.penguin.co.uk/readers

The Registrar General – Births, Deaths & Marriages
For certified copies of marriage and birth certificates
Tel: 0151 471 4200

Relate
To find your nearest Relate Centre, call 01788 573241, consult your phone book, or visit the Website: www.relate.org.uk

Solicitors Family Law Association
P O Box 302, Orpington, Kent BR6 8QX
Tel: 01689 850227 Website: www.sfla.co.uk

Recommended Reading

The Anti-Aging Bible
Advice on what to eat to stay healthy, fit and youthful for both men and women. Earl Mindell (Souvenir Press)

Breaking Up Without Falling Apart
A guide to separation & divorce in Scotland
Anne Hall Dick (B&W Publishing)

Choosing A Better Life
A step-by-step guide to building the future you want.
Hilary Jones & Frank Gilbert (How To-Pathways)

The Relate Guide to Loving in Later Life
A sensible and sensitive approach to relationships for older people. Marj Thoburn & Suzy Powling (Vermillion)

The Relate Guide to Starting Again
A valuable guide to building a new social life.
Sarah Litvinoff (Vermillion)

Secrets of Relationship Success
Written by a matrimonial lawyer to show why relationships fail and how to stop it happening (again)
Vanessa Lloyd Platt (Vermillion)

Take Time For Your Life
A practical guide offering a seven-step programme for creating the life you want. Cheryl Richardson (Bantam)

Where's Daddy?
A guide to coping with the impact of divorce on children
Jill Curtis & Virginia Ellis (Bloomsbury)

The Which? Way To Buy, Sell & Move House
How to manage your move with minimal stress and expense
Alison & Richard Barr (Which? Books)

The Which? Guide to Living Together
An essential guide for anyone co-habiting
Imogen Clout (Which? Books)

WLTM: The Dating Game
The definitive guide to using dating and introduction services
for the over 40s
Suzanne Ruthven and Polly Langford (ignotus)

Index

Relaxing: 166–172,
Religion: 27-30, 105,
Re-marriage: 187-190,
Renting Property: 125-126,
Revenge: 117-120,

Self-esteem: 172-174,
Sex: 18, 23, 45, 157, 187,
Shares: 64-65,
Special Procedure: 37-38,
Solicitors: 27, 35-50,
Statistics: 12-15, 35,

Telephone Life-line: 138-140,

Violence: 109-121,
Vive Magazine: 11,

Wills: 140-141,
Women's behaviour: 17, 30,
54, 117,

Alphard
LifeStyle